We Lived It
and Laughed
Tales of Chuluota, Florida

Mark Perrin

Cover photo: Mark Perrin
Editor: P.C. Zick
Contact Author: map32327@aol.com

ISBN-13: 978-1546789963
ISBN-10: 1546789960

DEDICATION

This is dedicated to the people who formed my first tribe and to those who now make up my second tribe and encouraged me to write these stories down. You all have enhanced my life and I thank you all.

CONTENTS

Introduction   2

The Swing   7

A Trip Back in Time   10

The Carnivorous Armadillos   15

The Cannonball   19

Some Chuluota Ingenuity   22

The Deer Hunt   27

A Billy Story   31

Another Billy Story   34

Ray Gordon   37

Canned Goods   40

First Impressions   43

The Burning   46

The Charlie Chips Can   48

First Cars   52

Screwing One Around   56

A Few More Oz Stories   61

Penis Stories   69

The Miami Trip   77

Right Out of the Movies   87

Chuluota Tough   98

Picking Up Granny   102

The Lake Shark   106

Cops   110

Final Thoughts   121

About the Author   124

ACKNOWLEDGMENTS

First, I would like to thank the friends and relatives who over the years encouraged me to write these stories down. For upon hearing these stories told, they deemed them good enough not to let them fade away and die in the dust of time. I, too, agree. Secondly, I would like to thank Sandy Tedder, who so generously gave her time to review, helped ready these stories for publication and gave me answers to my computer questions, which were constant. And she always gave me words of encouragement. I would also like to thank the universe for having me cross paths with Patricia Zick. Patricia is a published author and professional editor who has helped with many other books. She graciously agreed to edit this collection of short stories and to turn it into a much more readable work. Last, I am thankful for the people who surrounded me in my early years and who served as the characters starring in these stories and in many more. You are my first tribe. I have long since moved away and now hang and interact with a different tribe. However, I still know the language and customs of my first tribe, and on occasion, still visit Chuluota. I am welcomed amongst them when I do. For this, I am grateful. It is nice to belong.

INTRODUCTION

Some say the town was started, and then came the store that sold beer. Others say the store that sold beer was built, and the town grew up around it. Time has passed, and sands have shifted, and now no one knows for sure. But all agree, one couldn't survive without the other. They called the place Chuluota, pronounced "Chew-lee-o-ta."

I did time there, some hard, some not. I spent more than twenty years in Chuluota and still get drawn back from time to time. You could say, I grew up there, but that wouldn't be exactly true, for either me and the other people with whom I did time. We never have truly grown up. It seems to be an ongoing process.

This book contains a collection of some of the true stories or incidents I either witnessed or that were told to me and were verified. There is no chronological order or degree of importance these people played in my life. I find myself telling the stories of all the people I knew, not just the core group I hung out with the most. Also, there is no intent to make fun of or belittle the people mentioned in these stories. I'm not judging anyone. I'm just retelling some good stories. I wrote these stories without going into details of the highly dysfunctional families most of my peers and I experienced. I'd rather not relive the details and possibly take away from what I think are mostly humorous stories. I just want it to be known that always in the background there were a lot of screwed-up home lives in that time and place. These hardships led to self-medicating and very little supervision. You take these ingredients and throw them in the blender with a boring town, and you can come out with some interesting results. I'm not sure why there was such a high level of screwed-up family lives in this small town. Maybe it was no higher than any other place, but somehow, we recognized this dysfunction in others, which drew us closer together. Some Chuluota cast members had what I consider fairly normal home lives and chose to run with us. Not many, but some. So, some of the stories have nothing to do with our family lives. They just happened to bored teenagers.

Chuluota is a small town located in central Florida halfway between Orlando and Titusville. The name Chuluota, like many Florida places, is Native American, and has been translated by white men to mean either "land of lakes and pines" or the more accepted, "foxes den." There's really no telling which one is correct, and there's a good chance some white man was way off the mark. After the Civil War, many southerners lost all they had and were looking for a new start. Some early settlers came from the Carolinas and settled in the area. They lived mostly a rural farming and hunting lifestyle. By the late 1800s, the citrus industry was beginning to grow in the area and began to replace the turpentine and timber industries that were on the way out. Chuluota continued to stay very rural and very lightly populated. In the 1920s, Mr. Henry Flagler ran his railroad line through the town, but it continued to remain very lightly populated. The passengers on the train probably weren't impressed with the smallness of the town coupled with its location three miles from the edge of the earth, so they never bothered getting off the train.

Moving forward to the 1950s, three men from up north—I believe from Michigan—decided to build a retirement community. How they found or decided on Chuluota, I'm not sure. They laid out and built seven streets with Chuluota's Lake Cathryn near the center. It became the focal point of town. There were two other smaller lakes within the seven street boundaries. The developer brought his own builder. He, with the help of only a couple of other people along the way, including his son, built the majority of the homes. For the most part, they were small, concrete-block homes with shallow sloping, hot-tar roofs along with jalousie windows. These homes were built on small lots and were intended to be very affordable. On Lake Cathryn, they also created a small beach area, a two-tiered dock that went out into the lake. They built swing sets and a shuffle board court. For a small yearly fee, the residents got access to these things, plus swimming lessons, if they wanted. I learned to swim there.

Older retired people bought homes and moved into the area. Many came from out of state. My grandparents were among them. They moved there from Mississippi in 1959 or 1960. My parents had already moved to Coco Beach from St. Louis when I was only six months old in late 1959. My dad, who was an engineer, had been hired to work on some of the early space shots in the Mercury Program. He soon bought land just outside of Chuluota in the woods on a small lake. He had a house built, and we moved there when I was three-and-a-half years old.

I have an older sister, Sandy, and an older brother, Larry. We all lived in this house until my parents divorced when I was twelve. They should have divorced many years before, but times were different then and that is a whole other story. The house in the woods was sold not too long after the divorce. My sister, who was eighteen, went out on her own when they divorced and moved to the Orlando area. My brother went with my father, and they lived in a small house on Fourth Street in Chuluota. I went with my mother, and we lived in a small house on Seventh Street.

While retirees were some of Chuluota's first main inhabitants in the 1950s, younger families began to move in also, mostly because of the location near Orlando when Disney started his empire in the late 1960s. Chuluota's houses were affordable for young couples just starting out. I would say there was an almost fifty-fifty ratio between elderly retirees and younger families by the time I moved from the woods to Seventh Street in Chuluota sometime around 1971.

Businesses were now coming to places not too distant. They included Cape Canaveral, Disney, Martin Marietta, along with all the businesses that come with supporting the people who work at these places. We also had all the cattle, citrus, and produce operations that were already established in and around Chuluota. There was a great mixing of diverse backgrounds and education levels.

While we still lived in the woods, we had gotten to know some of the other kids who lived in Chuluota through school or by playing sandlot football and baseball. Some of them came from the woods about a half mile away. So, when I first moved into downtown Chuluota, it was a little exciting. I now lived closer to people I knew and began meeting others, along with girls, which I didn't know too much about before then. Closer is a big deal when you're a kid and only have your feet, or perhaps a bicycle, to get around.

My parents soon remarried other people. My father married a very nice woman, who, if I ever found any fault with, was too nice. Not a bad fault to have. She had been a nun at one time, just to give you an idea. My father passed away not too long after his remarriage. I was nearly fourteen when he passed. My mother remarried a man who was retired from the Navy. My parents, all their peers, and my aunt and uncles were from the World War II generation.

My new stepfather liked to drink as much, if not more, than my mother and her friends. That's how they met. It created a dysfunctional upbringing, which I shared with many of my friends. Again, I don't want to go into detail at this time. I just want you to understand why I was without much supervision, and why I self-medicated and made some poor decisions. I believe my peers and I wanted to numb our pain as we raised one another. We found a way to bury our screwed-up home life with laughter. For the most part, we succeeded. We survived until adulthood without dying or going to prison, though a lot of us came close on both accounts.

These stories begin around 1971 or 1972, and mostly after I'm living on Seventh Street in Chuluota with my mother and stepfather. My father had passed away by then, and my brother finished out his senior year of high school and had started college. So, I didn't have a lot of interaction with my family besides my mother and stepfather. This is the real beginning of my living in Chuluota and the hardcore interaction with the people who lived there. The stories and events I describe take place throughout the seventies and into the early eighties. By 1977, I had moved out on my own, though I still lived in town.

The little community beach area of Lake Cathryn, the shuffle board courts, swing set, and two-tiered dock had all been abandoned by the time I was a teenager. They were only in service and maintained for a few years. However, they continued to be functional for a time and were a favorite hangout for my generation., especially the swimming area.

When we were growing up, we referred to three generations, but not in the traditional sense. We referred to generations as the group of kids who were just a few years older, our group, and the group behind us who were only a few years younger. There was quite a bit of intermingling of the ages through the years. However, the group I ran with would often mention and be aware of these group references. I'm not sure why, maybe the age thing was, or at least supposed to be, a big deal. The people who were truly the generation before us—our parents—for the most part, were irrelevant. They abandoned us. They didn't need us or want us, and we didn't need them. At least, that's the attitude we carried. Through it all, we made our own family—our tribe. We formed a bond that still exists to this day, and can be felt from many miles away.

The names of the people mentioned in these stories have been changed to hopefully keep me from being sued, or more importantly, from being beat up.

THE SWING

Calvin Tucker. He was just a few years older and from what we called "the older generation" ahead of mine. He was what I consider a real hippie. He was of age for Woodstock, Vietnam, and real potent acid. My generation remembered these things all too well. We were just a little too young to participate.

Calvin, for the most part, didn't run with my group, but being from a small town, we all knew one another. Also, he had a younger sister who hung out with us some, plus some other girls he ran with had younger sisters that we knew—all a part of that small-town intermingling.

As my generation got older, and we started partying, we often had organized parties in the woods. These were often good enough that the older guys and girls would come, too. Often times, there were big fires, and people would play guitars and such. Calvin was one of the guitar players. I tried playing some, too, so Calvin and I had a connection. I worked a job with him for about three months when I was eighteen. Riding with him every day, back and forth, I got to know him better. Thus, I learned a couple of his stories.

One day while riding home from work, he asked me, "Did I ever tell you about me going all the way around on the swing up by the lake?"

I'm sure my eyebrows probably went up some, as a visualization and a huge wave of skepticism came into my mind. "Why no, I don't think you have."

The community area was run publicly and was maintained only for a few years before being abandoned. But it remained functional for quite a few years afterwards, especially the beach area. The swings were built very well with steel pipes embedded in concrete at the base. The seats were hung with chains. Anyway, Calvin told me, as a kid, he often went to the swings by the lake after school and was always seeing how high he could get.

Swing high, not drug high. That would come later. Not much later, but later. As kids, many of us had done the same thing. He became obsessed with the thought of going all the way around on the swing. That's right, over the bar, for a complete revolution. He—and anyone else who has tried—quickly learned when you get to a certain point, slack gets in the chain, and you come back down somewhat straight and sometimes rather hard. After much pondering, and with determination, he figured out if he could enlist the help of a couple of large guys, he might be able to pull it off. Thus, giving him legendary status in Chuluota lore. For whatever that may be worth.

The plan was to get swinging and use the two guys at just the right time to give him a really hard shove to send him beyond the point where slack got in the chain, which would allow him to make a complete revolution—much like a gymnast on the high bar.

Calvin recruited a couple of guys, who he deemed idiots for not believing in his plan. He told me for several afternoons after school they had tried various methods. Sometimes, they would do all the pushing of his swinging activities to get their timing down better, and other times, they would just provide a final big shove at what they thought was the crucial time.

One day, after several attempts, they were going to once again call it quits, but then decided they would give one final try for the day. So, they made it a good one. He told me he had swung about as high as he was going to get and had just begun his upward motion, when his two enlistees hit him with a well-timed, strong, together as one, shove. He said he went higher than ever before and got right over the swing bar when gravity kicked in and brought slack in the chains. Calvin fell from the sky like a sack of potatoes and landed on the bar, breaking his arm instantly, but he had the presence of mind to "fall on the good side," as he told me.

By falling over on "the good side," it officially counted as going all the way over the swing. When he told me this story while driving down the road, I remembered he turned and looked directly at me.

"Do you know, those idiots told me I couldn't do it," he told me.

I thought, but didn't say, "Yeah Calvin, they really were some idiots."

Still skeptical, I did ask one of his so-called swing helpers one day if this was a true story. He laughed and told me he hadn't thought of that in many years.

"Oh yeah, we got lucky with the well-timed final shove, and Calvin came straight down and hit the bar and broke his arm," he said. "Pretty sure it knocked the breath out of him, too, when he hit the ground. We thought he might be bad hurt, until the first words he said was something about falling on the good side, so it counted."

In Chuluota, it seemed to me that many of the people had what I think is a very unique and downright hilarious way of looking at things. When Calvin told me this story, he had two main points he wanted to get across to me. One, he wanted to brag a little for having gone all the way around on a swing, feeling quite confident I didn't know anyone else who had. Two, he wanted to let me know the other two Chuluota guys were idiots for not believing in his plan. Him breaking his arm was very secondary and hardly worth mentioning. I find this way of seeing things very humorous, and yet, kind of common among the people I was running with. Story one—I always thought this story was worthy of repeating.

A TRIP BACK IN TIME

At a very early age, I had a great interest in history. I'm not sure why, but it led me to search for and collect old bottles by the time I turned ten. I didn't really know what I was doing and most knowledge was self-taught. I only knew the older the bottle, the better. I mainly sought out the old surface dumps in the woods. I hoped to find bottles from the 1800s, or at least, cork-topped bottles. Most bottles had gone to screw tops by the 1930s. I asked people I met, or already knew, if they knew where I could find these old bottles. Sometimes, people would tell me of places. Usually, if I found bottles there, they would be newer than what I sought.

One day, I asked a guy in my Boy Scout troop if he knew where I could find any old bottles.

"Sure," Jake Harper said. "The lake behind my house."

"Are they old, are they cork-top?" I asked as I usually did whenever anyone claimed to know of a spot.

Jake assured me they were old. He told me where he lived, and though it was about three miles from my house, I made plans to go. I either walked or rode a bike, I don't remember now it's been so long. But I think I must have walked, for I clearly remember going slowly up the final driveway. I also remember it was a warm afternoon after school. When you live in a small town, everyone knows everyone else, so I knew the Harper family had two boys and a couple of girls. I ended up getting to know the two boys much better later on, but when I went seeking old bottles, I didn't know them all that well. Billy was a couple of years older than me, and Jake was about a year younger. They were part of an older time in Florida. Some folks would call them Florida Crackers. They all talked with the heavy twang of the rural Florida woods. The day I went to their house for the first time, I was about twelve years old. I found the old wooden house at the end of a small narrow dirt road, in the middle of an orange grove, up against a large lake.

At some point—I would say within a hundred yards of the house—I walked through some kind of a time warp. As I entered the small clearing around the house, I was transported back fifty years, from 1970 to about 1920. In the side yard, a large man worked on a tractor. A very large man. At least six-foot-four and 240 pounds of solid, no flab man. He wore overalls, a hat, and no shirt. I assumed it was Mr. Harper. As I came up the dirt-road-turned driveway, he looked up, took me in, and went right back to work on the tractor without saying a word. As I continued, I saw Billy in the back shodding a horse. He was cussing quite a bit while doing so. He was probably fourteen or fifteen back then. I didn't see Jake or anyone else, so I continued toward the house. As I walked up on the front porch heading towards the door, I heard a large commotion just inside the house. Suddenly, the front door burst open. A small lady appeared cussing in that Florida Cracker accent and kicking chickens out the door.

"Who in the hell let the son of bitchen chickens back in the house?" she yelled as she kicked at the hens. Then she looked up and saw me— a skinny twelve-year-old with a shocked look on his face.

She looked me dead in the eye and said, "Who in the wide world of sports are you?"

"I-I'm Mark Perrin, ma'am. Jake told me to come by to see some old bottles." I stuttered my words.

"Old bottles? What kind of old bottles?"

"Some old cork-topped bottles he said was in the lake out back."

"What do you want with those? You can't take 'em to the store for two cents like you can the coke bottles."

"No, ma'am, I just collect old bottles." She immediately felt sorry for me.

"Boy, who's your people?" She now felt sorry for them, too.

I was relieved when Jake appeared.

"Go show him those bottles although I ain't sure what he wants with bottles you can't get anything from," she said when Jake asked if he could take me down to the lake. "But come back, you got chores to do."

Jake and I headed down to the lake just out back. I was glad to get away, for my twelve-year-old mind had taken in a lot very quickly.

Down at the lake, just to one side of a small dock, sure enough there were some corked-top bottles down in the water. Not a lot but a few. I don't remember too much about the bottles because they were not real old. Probably from the 1920s. But they were corked-top, and I wasn't being picky in the early days.

I waded out and got all the bottles I could see. I was putting my shoes back on, up on shore, when Billy, Jake's brother, appeared. He was looking over his shoulder, so I figured he must have snuck off from doing chores.

"Did Jake show you our ski boat?" Billy asked.

"I don't see a ski boat," I said.

"It's tied up at the end of the dock," Billy said. "Come on, we'll show you."

Sure enough, tied up at the end of dock was a Harper-style ski boat. It consisted of a twelve-foot wooden row boat. Bolted and strapped down on the back of it a motor far too large for a boat that size. A twenty-five horsepower motor attached to a small wooden row boat. I was impressed.

"You got to have a motor that large to get up enough speed to pull a skier," Billy said.

He then explained why there were concrete blocks piled in the front of the boat.

"It keeps the boat from flipping over when the motor is cranked wide open. It took a lot of trial and error to figure out the right number."

I could just imagine. Then he informed me because of all the weight pushing the boat down in the water, it took the boat a while to reach the speed needed to pull up a skier.

"I damn near drowned a time or two," he continued. "I was pulled all over the lake, being drug through the water, and Jake couldn't get up to speed enough to pull me up on the skies." He smiled. "But we figured out that problem, too."

"Jake get in the boat and start it up," Billy directed. "We'll show Mark how our ski boat works."

So, Jake started the boat, and Billy sat on the end of the dock wearing two water skis with a coil of rope in his lap.

"Hit it, Jake, hit it," Billy said when he was all set.

Jake hit it, and the boat took off from the dock. I watched the coil of rope in Billy's lap peel out. The rope hit its end after rolling out one hundred feet or so, and Billy was snatched off the dock. He landed on his skis, and, by God, he was skiing. This was just sheer country ingenuity.

There weren't many skiers back then, or many ski show tourist attractions for them to have learned this trick.

All these years later, I still remember the sight. An old wooden row boat, with a big motor, concrete blocks piled in the front, all being driven by an eleven-year-old boy, while his older brother skied on the back. These boys never played organized sports, but they were very athletic and coordinated, especially Billy.

As Jake brought the boat back to the dock, Mrs. Harper walked down to the lake, shaking her head. I'm sure she was wondering why the boys weren't doing chores, and I decided it was a good time to take my bottles and leave. She didn't say anything to me as I walked past.

She now knew me as the boy who took home old bottles you couldn't even cash in at the store. She felt sorry for me and my people.

THE CARNIVOROUS ARMADILLOS

My best friends growing up were Steve McAllister and Robert Osbourne. This story concerns their older brothers, John McAllister and Tom Osbourne

They were about three years older than us and much bigger than us. They played high school football and loved to pick on us and beat us in general for sport. They both went on to play college football at a 2-A college. John was a linebacker and Tom, a lineman.

John, Tom, my brother Larry, and many others their age, drank but didn't smoke pot or do drugs during their high school days. Those activities were for hippies. A pretty sharp line was drawn between the two. My peers and I would sometimes get beat up by our older brothers and their friends for smoking pot or just looking like we might smoke pot. Having long hair didn't help. However, lots of these older guys discovered pot and other drugs once they got out of high school. My brother didn't, but John and Tom did.

Robert Osbourne—better known simply as "Oz"—Slim Richardson, and me actually drove Tom and John to Elon College in North Carolina in Mrs. Osbourne's car. We helped them move into a dormitory full of football players. We got some very hard stares as we carried clothes and such into the building, for we were about sixteen, much smaller, and had longer hair. These guys were wondering if we could somehow be on the team. Of course, the few times someone would ask or talk to us, I would mention I played defensive back and was looking forward to hitting some people.

John and Tom joined a fraternity made up of a lot of college athletes. They started smoking pot and drinking, and generally enjoying the partying college life with their new fellow athletic friends. At this time—the mid-seventies—Florida was the Mecca for pot coming into the country. My friends and I were informed Chuluota Florida hippies, so we had connections.

John and Tom decided to bring some of their fraternity brothers to Florida for a weekend of partying and to get some pot. We probably had access to some of the best and cheapest. Or if nothing else, we were safe, honest, and could be trusted. They wouldn't have to worry about being ripped off or arrested. So, John and Tom and three or four of their big ole friends piled into a car and headed to Florida.

The three or four guys they were bringing weren't from Florida and didn't know much about it. Somewhere along the road near the Florida line, they spotted their first road-kill armadillo. The guys who knew nothing about Florida had never seen one before, dead or alive. For some reason, John mentioned that armadillos were carnivorous. They were skeptical, but Tom backed John up.

"You don't hear much about it because they're small, and usually, they are by themselves and are fairly timid," Tom told them. "However, sometimes they run in packs. If there are more than four in a pack, they'll start getting aggressive and take on larger animals. Packs of twelve or more will go for deer and the occasional human, too."

The guys were still kind of skeptical, but here were two Florida boys telling them this. As they drove on down I-95, they saw more and more dead armadillos. Sometimes they'd see two fairly close to one another. John and Tom would take the opportunity to point out those were probably part of a pack that had gotten hit by a car while chasing a deer or something.

That's the background for my brief story. Now fast forward to Saturday night. My friends and I met up with John, Tom, and their friends at Pooh Bear's house. Pooh Bear is better known as simply Pooh, but his real name is Paul Cooper. I often called him Hoop. For that is Pooh spelled backwards, and I was "different." Pooh was a ranger at a park in Chuluota with a lake and nature trails. Some of the trails had wooden walkways going through some really nice swamp land. The county furnished Pooh with a modest income and a small house in the park. Pooh also sold pot. We went there often.

Us local boys and the Florida newcomers were sitting   in Pooh's house smoking large amounts of pot and drinking large amounts of beer and bullshitting like we normally did. It was decided we needed to go for a walk through the park at night. We did this often, since Chuluota was a boring town. There was a lot of drinking, smoking, and walking around at night. A couple of people had flashlights. We never used flashlights unless deemed absolutely necessary, like for a spider encounter or some other serious matter.

There were a series of boardwalks that went through a section of the park with a small natural swamp. We walked down a wooden walkway about a hundred yards into the swamp when we heard a noise in the bushes right next to the walkway. Someone turned on a flashlight, and there was an armadillo right beside us next to the walkway. Of course, I didn't think anything of it, and I'm sure it barely registered in my stoned mind.

Before I knew what happened, one of the guys in front of me yelled—or more like screamed—then he turned around and proceeded to run right into and over me. It was one of the football frat boys named Mack. He was about six-feet-eight-inches tall and weighed close to two hundred and eighty pounds, they later told me. He played defensive end on the football team. He also played basketball for the school. At the age of sixteen, I probably weighed somewhere close to a hundred and forty pounds. I remember that I went over backwards hard on the boardwalk, with him shoving and stomping on me as he went. As I was going down, I got pissed, and I tried to grab him.

"It's only an armadillo," I screamed.

"I know, I know!" he screamed back, as he and his other stoned friends ran down the walkway.

I was hurt and confused as I tried to get up. I could now hear John and Tom laughing their asses off. When they quit laughing, they told us what they'd told those guys about the carnivorous armadillos. I think they had forgotten all about it until those guys ran off screaming on that stoned night walk.

After all these years, I still remember quite clearly being run over by this big defensive end trying to escape the carnivorous armadillos. At least he wasn't screaming "save yourself," but it was implied.

THE CANNONBALL

I first met Pooh when I was about ten. His uncle was married to my cousin. They threw a birthday party for one of their two small boys, and Pooh and his family were invited. Pooh, AKA Paul Cooper, has three brothers and two sisters. Pooh is a couple of years older than me, but we ran together quite a bit when I moved into Chuluota when I was twelve. There wasn't a lot of adult supervision at his house, same as me. My brother actually gave Paul his nickname name, Pooh Bear. One night my brother, Paul, and a couple of other guys had scattered and run (different story) to elude danger. After a short time, they reemerged when they thought it was again safe. They couldn't find Paul. Then they heard a voice. Paul had shinnied way up a large pine tree, which had no lower branches. My brother declared he looked like a big Pooh Bear up there in the tree. The name stuck.

Anyway, I hung quite a bit with Pooh over the years. There are many stories to tell. Pooh was a park ranger for a time at the only county park in Chuluota. In fact, it was a new park. It had been one of our more popular party places prior to the county taking over. It was on a nice large lake. Pooh had gotten the job mainly because he had applied, and he was an EMT. He had a brief career with the fire department, which again, is another story. The park job didn't pay much, but they provided an older small house to live in, and he had an assistant ranger who did most of the work.

My friends and I often visited Pooh at his park house. He usually had lots of spare time, and he often had or sold pot. I was around eighteen at the time of this story. Pooh was in his early twenties. We spent quite a few summer days drinking beer, smoking pot, and throwing Frisbees. We actually became fairly good at throwing Frisbees. Not much to brag about I guess. It didn't help the resume or count towards any college degree that I'm aware of. Can't remember any women ever being impressed, either. It was something to do while we were stoned, I suppose.

One day, a few friends and I were at Pooh's. One of the friends was Micky, who wasn't from Chuluota. He was from the nearby town of Geneva. He hung out with me and a few friends from time to time during my senior year in high school. So, Micky knew everyone, but he probably hadn't been to Pooh's often, or it could have even been his first time there. I don't remember. But I do remember, we had been in Pooh's house for a while smoking large amounts of pot and drinking beer.

We decided to go outside and play with the Frisbees as we often did. We all stepped out on the open front porch. We stretched and let our glazed eyes adjust to the sunlight. It just so happened that on this front porch was a large eighty-pound cannonball. It had been stolen from an historical place. I didn't do it, but I won't tell who did. Out of the corner of my eye, I saw Micky suddenly move forward. Before anyone could say anything, Micky kicked that eighty-pound cannonball with everything he had. He looked up and out, expecting to see, what I guess he thought was, a black kickball sailing off the porch. It took half a second for the pain to register.

Sadly, Micky did break his big toe, and I now see that it's not funny. However, it took a moment for this event to register in our stoned minds, but then we all noticed the cannonball as it slowly rolled its way all the way off the porch. It made a dull "wump, wump, wump" noise as it went. Being of the Chuluota mindset and being quite stoned, we found this to be hilariously funny. We did take care of Micky. We applied first aid—Pooh being an EMT was once again found handy—and gave him pain killers of whatever sort we had. It might have only been liquor and more pot. I don't remember.

There were jokes made as we set Micky up in the shade and proceeded to throw Frisbees.

"What the hell were you thinking?" I asked.

"Who the hell keeps a cannonball on their porch?" Mickey barked back.

"You're going to pay for that damn cannonball if it's damaged," Pooh said.

After all these years, I still remember the noise that cannonball made as it slowly rolled off the porch. There is a good chance that Micky, to this day, holds some kind of record for having kicked an eighty-pound cannon ball farther than anyone, ever.

SOME CHULUOTA INGENUITY

As you can tell, the earlier stories are filled with tales of Chuluota ingenuity, such as Calvin figuring out how to go all the way over the bar on the swing, and the Harper boys figuring how they could water ski with what they had or could borrow. I have plenty more to tell.

Pooh Bear and his brothers, while teenagers, found a couple of rolls of brick wallpaper at their house. For those who don't know or don't remember, wallpaper with a brick pattern printed on it was used some in the sixties. The brothers had the great idea of stretching it across a dirt road at night on a curve. Again, there wasn't a whole lot of supervision from adults for many of us. I always thought this was a fairly impressive idea. I can say this because no one got hurt. They found if they ran fishing line across the road really tight about three feet high and fastened the wallpaper to it, it looked pretty damn good. Late at night when you're driving down a country road, and you suddenly come upon a brick wall while going around a curve, well, you can imagine. Even if you're sober, your mind can't compute fast enough that there shouldn't be a brick wall going across a road. A couple of cars did come by late that night. They slammed on their brakes and then drove harmlessly through the brick wallpaper wall.

The boys laughed, but remained hidden. No telling what the drivers thought. If I had been driving, I'd like to think I would have been impressed. Even though my blood pressure would have risen. The boys then ran more fishing line and attached more wallpaper, and they were back in business. After a few more cars with very similar results, a car—the last of the night—slammed on the brakes and went into a ditch. There was no damage to the car or driver, but the boys called it a night. I always thought this story was worth retelling because it shows Chuluota ingenuity—harmless for the most part.

These next two stories I witnessed firsthand. One day, and I'm not sure where, I was standing next to Vicky Sutton. Vicky is from Chuluota. I believe she had a fairly normal home life and didn't hang with us much in the early days. She started to run with us mostly after high school. She ended up marrying one of my best friends, Steve McCallister. She probably saved his life, or at least, kept him from going to prison. But alas, this story is about her. One day when I was standing near her, she opened her purse. I could see the handle of what looked like a big gun.

"Vicky, is that a pistol you have in your purse?" I asked.

"No. I was scared to carry a pistol without a concealed weapons permit. So, I got this flare gun instead."

I thought that was a great idea. I'm sure it would still be considered a concealed weapon. However, I thought an average cop would let her go just for the ingenuity.

I could imagine someone trying to rob or take Vicky's car and her pulling out her flare gun. First, if you were to look down the barrel of it, it'd scare the hell out of you. It must have been at least fifty calibers, which is a very large opening. Then if she pulled the trigger, you'd see a bright flash followed by a loud roar. Then if it hit you, no telling what you'd see, hear, and feel. I'm sure it wouldn't be good though. After all of these years, I have never seen or heard of anyone packing a flare gun.

This next story was what, I thought, was a great idea by another Chuluota woman. I witnessed this one, too, and I was quite impressed.

MARK PERRIN

This story took place, of all places, at the Contemporary Hotel in Disney World. My high school class had their prom there, but I didn't go. My class only ever had one reunion, and that was our tenth. However, the class behind mine is more responsible and has had several. They have invited my class and the one behind them to a couple of their reunions. I believe this one was their twentieth. So, it would have been my twenty-first. Making me and my classmates around thirty-eight years old. They decided to have it at the Contemporary Hotel, they said, because my class prom was held there. In reality, I think some of the women who were helping plan the event, just wanted to dress up. Contemporary Hotel is fairly nice and respectable. Women wore evening gowns for the most part. Most guys wore nice shirts and pants with a few suits thrown in.

Now my guess, only a guess mind you, was that the planners were worried about not having enough people attend to pay for the banquet room, food, and DJ. So, they got lax on the requirements to attend. If you were in the same class as one of the three invited but didn't necessarily graduate with your class, you could go, too. This opened the door for quite a few Chuluota peers who were supposed to have graduated with these three classes, but for one reason or another had quit school. And come they did.

The reunion was being held in one big banquet room in the hotel. There was a stage with a microphone, a cash bar, dance floor, and a bunch of big round tables. At least ten to twelve could sit at a table. By this time, I hadn't drunk alcohol in more than eight years. It had been time for me to quit. I had kept in touch with a couple of the Chuluota people, but no longer lived there, and I found myself a little reluctant to sit with them, for I knew the dangers. Guilt by association, you know. I ended up sitting next to Vicky, the woman who carried a flare gun, for I liked her and knew she was probably the safest of the group. I don't think she was packing at the Contemporary Hotel. She was now divorced from Steve who was there with two of his sisters and assorted other Chuluotians. They all seemed to get along fine.

I told Vicky when I sat next to her I wasn't sure if I ought to sit at the table with the Chuluota heathens, for several were already quite buzzed and at least one had brought his own hidden liquor bottle, thus avoiding the high price of the cash bar. There were lots of ingredients for things to go bad or at least get embarrassing as hell. She smiled at me and patted the back of my hand.

"You sit right here and trust me, this will be hilarious."

So, with that, I did relax and just changed my attitude and sat back to watch. Vicky was right, pretty damn funny evening.

Now I'm not going to bore you with the minor things Chuluota people did during the evening. I will say that security did come in and watch the table and that area most of the night. I also know some of them had rooms rented in the hotel, and they ended up getting kicked out later in the night. The whys I do not know for thankfully I wasn't with them. I do know that the Chuluota world and the family-oriented Disney World are light years apart.

Early in the night, the class president—the emcee for the night—got on the microphone. He welcomed everyone and pointed out the disposable cameras on the tables. He asked people to take pictures of one another at their tables during the evening. At the end of the night, the cameras would be gathered and later the film would be developed. Then a scrapbook would be made from the pictures, which could be purchased by anyone interested. As soon as he made the announcement, Kaitlin McCallister, Steve's sister, leaned forward at our table.

"Here's what we do," she began. "We take the cameras in the bathrooms and take nudies of one another. Shoulders and below, no head shots. When we've filled up the cameras, we sneak them onto other people's tables so there is no provable way they can be linked back to us."

I was impressed with the ingenuity and incredible speed she thought of this. Mind you, this is way before people had cell phones, and people taking selfies and such. I told her I was impressed and only a little embarrassed I hadn't thought of it myself. She wasn't overly proud or anything because it was simply and blatantly obvious what needed to be done. It's the Chuluota mind set. Now sadly, I do not know if any of the picture taking happened. If so, again sadly, I wasn't part of it.

I would like to think it did happen on some scale and that the scrapbook committee was a little surprised. Maybe not too surprised, for they did invite trouble. Perhaps they thought after twenty years, Chuluota people had grown up and matured. Silly people.

THE DEER HUNT

In Chuluota, there was always a mixing of the worlds. It may have been slight, but a mixing nonetheless. There were the old country men who were cattle ranchers, along with the old time orange grove owners. Since it was very rural with lots of trees, lakes, and ponds, many of my friends and I fished and hunted in the surrounding woods. We knew some of the country folk through these activities. Also, just plain being a small town meant we knew one another a little or at least recognized each other. Then as we got older, a few of us worked for these people or hung out with their children. Some were even hippies like us.

Chuluota had seven streets, plus there were homes scattered haphazardly throughout the wooded area outside of those seven streets. It also had one store, one gas station, one post office, three churches, and, by God, a bar that sat a mile out of town. The bar was occupied by mostly older local country men, who had no use for us, for the most part. We were long-haired hippies. Which was fine with us, we didn't want to go in the bar and listen to their old country juke box crap, anyway. However, when I was about eighteen, new owners bought the place. They had two sons and two daughters. The daughters were cute, about our age, and just plain new to the area. So, pretty soon some friends and I began going to the bar some. We were tolerated. Mrs. McAllister, Steve's mom, worked there quite a bit. I had grown

27

up with her large family. She liked me. Steve and I ran together for a number of years. Because of our relationship with Mrs. McAllister, we were accepted by most of the older country guys. After some time, I would like to think, that they even mostly liked us, once they got to know us. So, our worlds mixed with a combination of country, rednecks, hippie, and in between.

A guy named Rodger Jamison, better known as RJ, along with Pete Harper—a very large man, the father of Billy and Jake, the country water skiers—and perhaps a couple of other people, leased five hundred plus acres right outside of Chuluota for hunting. For the most part, it was very thick and dense with pines, palmettos, and titi thickets. A two-lane paved highway ran the length of its southern boundary. A mostly straight dirt road ran for about two miles on its northern boundary. This road made a ninety-degree turn on both ends, going back to the two-lane paved highway.

Because of the thick overgrowth, and just plain because they liked to do it, they mostly hunted this block of woods with dogs. For the most part, they would set dogs out on the southern boundary, and hopefully, drive deer to the northern side along the two-mile dirt road. There they would have hunters spaced apart. I was invited to join them a time or two. I remember driving down that road one day during one of their hunts. I saw quite a few hunters. Most I knew or at least recognized. I wasn't really into dog hunting. Then, when I saw that many of the hunters weren't spaced too far apart and that some had shot guns, but many also had rifles, well, it looked pretty darn dangerous to me. There was only a small area between the road and the thick woods. One would have to be quick to recognize if the deer was a buck and get a shot off while the deer was in front of the hunter. It looked to me like a shot could get fired down that road—instead of into the woods—pretty easily. I passed on joining those activities.

One day, I got word that a friend of mine had been shot during a dog hunt down there. I found out quickly that it wasn't life threatening or too serious. But shot nonetheless. The friend was Troy Burner and the shooter was Jake Harper—the country boy driving the ski boat when he was about eleven. Jake was now a young adult as was Troy. Jake had shot him with double-ought buck. For those who don't know, 12-gauge double-ought buck has nine pieces of lead in each shell about as big as a small 22-bullet. It's fired out of a shotgun. It is very effective and very deadly at close range. Not so much the farther you get away. Jake had hit Troy with two of the nine pieces. One hit him in the hip, the other right in the ass.

I ran into Troy not too long after the shooting. After finding out how he was, I asked for the story, for I didn't know any of the details. Troy proceeded to tell me.

"Hell, yeah, the son of the bitch shot me."

I detected a little bitterness. I'm astute that way. He proceeded to tell me the rest of the story.

"I was standing on the road spaced apart from a lot of the others. I could hear the dogs getting closer. Then I could hear the deer out in front of the dogs, breaking through the brush, out in front, but between where Jake and I were standing. I threw my gun up as the deer suddenly appeared out of the brush but still out in front of us. I quickly saw that it was a doe [not legal to take], and I lowered my gun. As the deer kept running and getting closer to cross the road we were standing on, I noticed Jake still had his gun up and was rapidly trying to line up on the deer. I realized, damn, Jake is going to shoot. The deer was getting real close to being directly in between us. I just dropped to the ground. Jake fired and the shot went over me and missed the deer, too. I jumped up to cuss Jake and noticed the deer had spun around and was coming back across the road." He shook his head and continued his tale.

"Damn Jake was still aiming. I hit the ground again. Sure enough, Jake fired again, and the shot went over me. The deer was also missed again. This time I was taking no chances. I jumped up and ran across the road. Then, damn, I noticed, by God, the deer had once again spun around and was now running back across the road to the same side I was now on. Jake was again aiming, trying to follow the deer. I, too, was trying to run but was too late. Jake fired."

"What the hell happened then?" I asked.

"What the hell do you think happened? I suddenly felt my ass and hip light up. I went about ten feet straight up in the air, and my gun went flying. As soon as I hit the ground, I began crawling towards my gun. I was going to kill the son of a bitch."

Jake realized what he had done and ran towards Troy. But Jake ran right past him and grabbed Troy's gun and placed it a safe distance away. Jake wasn't the sharpest knife in the drawer, but he wasn't stupid, either.

The others ran to Troy and patched him up, gave him a beer, and took him to the hospital.

This story could have been tragic, but it wasn't. To hear Troy tell it, it was downright funny. I thought it worthy of repeating. By the way, the deer ran off unharmed. The deer may have thought this story humorous, too.

A BILLY STORY

I have quite a few Billy Harper stories. Not sure how many I'll tell. To say that he was and is quite a character is a vast understatement. Billy was the older of the two Harper boys, the water skiers. Billy was tragically shot and paralyzed from the chest down while he was in his early twenties. I don't remember his exact age anymore.

After his initial recovery, it didn't seem to slow Billy down much. It seems he did more crazy things than most people do or even hear about in a lifetime. This is a story of the time I saw Billy with his first car after being shot and paralyzed.

It was one late afternoon, and I was hanging out in front of the little store, a place where many of my friends and I met and hung out and wasted countless hours. A red and black Ford Mach I came rumbling into the parking lot. It pulled up to where I was standing. It was Billy Harper driving. He stuck his head out the window.

"Check out my new ride," he said.

"Looks good," I said. "Bet it runs."

This car came from the factory with a 428-cobra jet motor, noted for horse power and speed, hence the rumbling when he pulled up. The name alone had to add an extra something to the power.

He told me he had ordered hand controls for the car, but they hadn't come in yet.

"I didn't want to wait, so I made this." He smiled and then held up a thirty-inch long piece of an inch-and-a-half diameter PVC pipe, with a PVC t-fitting glued to one end to make a handle. "Watch this."

Billy put the car in reverse and slammed the gas pedal down to the floor with one end of the PVC pipe. The motor screamed, smoke rolled off the back tires, and the car shot in reverse out into the parking lot. Billy then cut the wheel hard, and the car spun in a half circle with a cloud of blue smoke with the sound of its screaming motor and squealing tires filling the air.

The centrifugal force slung Billy off the steering wheel. He disappeared. Hard for Billy to stay upright with no feeling below his chest and only his arms and hands to hold onto the spinning steering wheel. The car was sliding sideways, tires screeching. Through the blue smoke, I saw a hand reach up and grab the wheel. Then Billy pulled himself upright again. The car came to stop, but only briefly.

Billy dropped the shifter into drive and slammed the gas pedal to the floor again using the PVC pipe. The motor screamed, tires squealed, and again another large cloud of blue smoke rolled off the back tires. This time the car was doing donuts but going forward as it spun. On about the second revolution, I saw Billy once again disappear as he got slung off the steering wheel. As the car once again began sliding sideways, I saw a hand reach up and grab the steering wheel. He then pulled himself back up behind the steering wheel once more.

Now this was all taking place around four or five o'clock in the early evening. There wasn't a lot of traffic coming in and out of the little store, mind you. Remember, Chuluota is a fairly rural town and all. But there were a few people stopping in after work and such, some with children. I'm sure they probably didn't understand. The people who ran the store probably weren't too shocked, for they had seen other craziness. Billy, I'm sure, didn't see anything wrong with it. Just a guy out in the parking lot showing off his car. Nothing going on here.

I remember Billy came idling back up to where I still stood.

"Come on, get in, we'll go for a ride."

Now I was probably around eighteen years old, give or take. I wasn't the brightest guy, and about half crazy myself at that stage of my life. However, I wasn't about to get in that car with Billy and his PVC driving stick.

After all of these years, I still remember that red and black Mach I sliding sideways in a cloud of blue smoke with no driver in sight, and then a hand reaching up and grabbing the wheel as the car was still sliding, and Billy pulling himself back up behind the wheel.

And he wanted me to get in and go for a ride.

ANOTHER BILLY STORY

This story was told to me shortly after it took place many years ago, by a good friend, Ray Gordon. I'll introduce and tell a Ray Gordon story or two soon. But for now, I had known Ray since elementary school, and he ran with us quite a bit. He married one of the Harper daughters.

The story takes place at the Harper place. They were no longer living in the time warp in the wooden house in the grove on a lake where the water skiing story took place. They eventually got a mobile home on some land on a dirt road. Billy, paralyzed, lived at home with his parents. My friend Ray was visiting with one of the Harper girls before they married.

Jake Harper pulled up to the house. Jake was the younger brother, the ski boat operator and the Troy shooter from earlier stories. Ray said that Jake came into the house and told them to come outside and check out his new motorcycle. I'm not sure if it was brand new, but it was new to Jake. I believe it was a Honda 350, a good running and fairly popular bike at the time.

Billy told Jake to let him drive his motorcycle.

"No, you can't drive my motorcycle," Jake told him.

"Why the hell not?" came the response.

"Because you're paralyzed, and you'll wreck it."

"I can drive your bike, and I ain't gonna wreck it."

"How the hell you going to drive it?" Jake asked.

"Just put it up on its center kick stand and lift me up on it, and I'll show you."

By the way, there were no parents witnessing this. I know Mrs. Harper was there, but in a back room.

Ray proceeded to tell me that Billy convinced Jake to let him drive his motorcycle. Ray said the bike was on its center kickstand, and he and Jake managed to pick Billy up out of his wheelchair and set him astraddle the motorcycle. Billy turned the key and hit the electric start button. The bike started. Billy then gave the bike gas with his right hand, held on, then leaned way down with his left hand and pushed the shifter down into first gear, then drove the bike off the kickstand. Anyone who has driven a car or a motorcycle without using a clutch knows this is a very tricky thing to do. It can be done, but it is definitely tricky. The vehicle tends to buck and wants to stall. After the initial take off, it's not too bad if you shift between gears not using a clutch. You let off the gas at the proper RPM and shift. It's still tricky, but not as tricky as the initial taking off. This is a very impressive and a skillful thing for a paralyzed person to do.

Ray said the bike wobbled, but Billy maintained it, and straightened it out. Billy drove the bike around the yard and then picked up speed. He let off the gas, leaned down, and shifted into second. Billy was now circling the mobile home. Ray said everyone was kind of surprised how smoothly everything was going, and Jake seemed somewhat relieved. Then Billy went on down the driveway and turned onto the dirt road. He started driving down the dirt road leaning down and shifting gears as needed. Then Billy drove out of sight.

Ray said they were all surprised but not totally shocked. After all, this was Billy, and they figured he'd return shortly. Jake was nervous about his motorcycle, but there was not a lot he could do. Ray told me they all went back into the house and more or less forgot about Billy.

Ray said that after a while, they heard this crash down at the other end of the mobile home. Everyone ran outside, including Mrs. Harper this time. The crash was down at the end of the trailer where she had been, and she couldn't help but hear it. Ray said they all ran down to the end of the trailer, and there was Billy with the motorcycle on top of him.

"Get the motorcycle off Billy," Mrs. Harper screamed. "Get the motorcycle off Billy. What the hell is Billy doing driving a motorcycle? For God's sake, he's paralyzed."

"What the hell did you do to my bike?" Jake yelled.

"Hell, I circled the trailer twice, wasn't no one out here," Billy screamed. "What the hell was I supposed to do, stop and put my leg down?"

He had a point.

Ray said they got the bike off Billy and put him back in his wheelchair. And neither him nor the motorcycle were hurt bad. Just a couple of scratches on both. To think, Ray married into this family, for a while anyway.

RAY GORDON

Now Ray Gordon came from what I consider a very normal home, an extreme rarity among my group of peers. His parents were a God-fearing, religious couple from Cairo, Georgia. Southern, religious, kind, and normal. We loved them, respected them, and therefore, left them alone. Ray ran with us quite a bit. He had an older brother and a younger sister. They stayed straight and religious and did not run with us. Now, Ray was different than most of us, because of his good, normal home life. He didn't ever smoke pot or do drugs that I am aware of. But he drank a lot with us and was around lots of drug use, mostly pot. He also kept his hair short, wore jeans and country-slanted shirts. He was one of the rarities that could and did bounce between worlds. He hung with country redneck ranchers and the local grove owners, but was also accepted among us heathen hippies and ran with us. Because of Ray's drinking and hanging with me and my group, I saw him do a few funny things.

One evening, quite a few of us were hanging out over at Pooh Bear's park ranger house, drinking and smoking large amounts of pot like we often did. Ray was among us. He had earlier in the day bought himself a nice felt cowboy hat. It was fairly expensive and quite the luxury for someone without a lot of money.

Ray had been bragging on his fine new hat most of the afternoon and evening. The more drinking he did the more he wanted to point out to all just how damn fine his hat was. I remember it was getting kind of old hearing about his fine hat, especially considering we were hippies and didn't give a damn about cowboy hats. I believe there were a few "fuck you and your hat, Ray," thrown his way.

We were sitting around quite buzzed telling stories and such. Ray, without saying a word, suddenly stood up off the couch, took two quick steps towards the door, whipped off his hat and threw up in it. I remember it took a couple of seconds for it to register to us all what we had just seen. Ray then proceeded to run outside where he continued getting sick. I remember how funny this struck us, kind of a karma thing for Ray bragging on his hat so much. Now, we were quite impressed that Ray was polite and considerate enough of Pooh not to throw up in his house. I believe Ray did manage to wash the hat out with a hose and salvage it. But it was never quite so special again.

Another time I remember, Ray, another person whose name I don't recall, and I were in a hole in the wall bar called Liars Lodge. It was at a fish camp where they also sold some food, and it was fairly safe in the daytime. Night time changed. There were some hardcore rednecks in the place, especially at night. They had the reputation of throwing people through windows about once a week. We were there in the daytime. I'm not sure why. It seems like we were meeting someone there. We had been drinking.

We were buzzed, but not over the top. We were about twenty years old at the time. The Liars Lodge Bar had napkins and condiments on a few tables, since they sold food. They also had pool tables, a bar, and juke box. Ray started playing with an A-1 Steak Sauce bottle that was on our table. He unscrewed the cap and popped the plastic insert out of the top. The plastic insert is what caused the sauce to dribble out as opposed to pour out. I was wondering why he had done this, when Ray suddenly put the bottle top in his mouth and downed the whole bottle of A-1 Steak Sauce.

"Ray, what the hell are you doing?" I asked.

"That wasn't shit." He then took two more bottles off other tables and drank those, too.

"That has got to be some kind of record," I announced.

I was, and still am, convinced that in the history of man no one else has probably ever drank three bottles of A-1 Steak Sauce.

Once, I saw Ray pick up one of our lighters while at a friend's house and casually light his own beard on fire. He quickly put it out, but not before creating a large cloud of very smelly smoke. Again, he had us saying, "Ray, what the hell?"

Drinking, boredom, and curiosity can make some people do some strange things. I'm sure Ray's parents could never have imagined.

CANNED GOODS

Now one would think most people wouldn't have too many stories involving canned goods. I am proud to say that I, too, do not have much to say about canned goods. However, I do have two brief stories.

Story one: I was over at a friend's house, Sammy Tallon. He wasn't a hardcore friend, but he ran with us for a couple of years after high school. I wish I could use his real name, for it, in itself, is rather comical. He had a nickname that he was much better known by, and in my opinion, better off using. For this book, though, we will call him Sammy Tallon.

I was at Sammy's one afternoon and asked to use his phone. The phone hung on the wall in the kitchen. I noticed while I was on the phone that there appeared to be a couple of bullet holes in one of the cabinets and in the wall nearby. I grew up in the woods, did a lot of target shooting, and still hunted some. I knew these things.

After I hung up, I asked Sammy about these holes.

"Oh, that. Yeah, they're bullet holes."

He opened up a couple of upper cabinets, and there were many more bullet holes on the inside of the cabinets. He told me his stepdad and a coworker—a fellow union iron worker—were drunk one evening and started target shooting the canned goods in the cabinets in the kitchen while sitting on the couch in the living room. To this day, I have never heard of anyone else ever doing this kind of target practice.

Story two: Mickey Cox, our cannonball kicker from an earlier story, told me this one shortly after it took place. Mickey was married three times by the age of thirty. This story is with wife number two. Mickey and his wife number two had been having some problems—if you knew Mickey you could just imagine—and she was in the process of leaving him. One evening, he came home to the apartment where they lived. He was pretty drunk, and his wife was there with one of her girlfriends packing up stuff and moving out.

Mickey said he was sitting on the couch for the most part, behaving and watching them pack up all the stuff. He said that a lot of the things she was packing, they had bought together, but that he was okay with it if she took them. He said he was fine when she took the TV, the VCR, stereo, the dishes. But then she started boxing up all the canned goods from the cabinets. Something about it seemed terribly unjust, and it hit him as just plain wrong. He thought that when someone was down, you just don't take his canned goods. Mickey said he began yelling at his wife about taking the canned goods, when he noticed a machete that happened to be in the living room with him—no telling why it was there. Sometime during his rant about the evils of taking a person's canned goods, he picked up the machete. Mickey said he made a loud noise and threw the machete at the opposite living room wall— his wife and her friend were safely in the kitchen packing canned goods. Much to Mickey's surprise, the machete spun in the air across the room and stuck perfectly in the wall. His wife and her girlfriend freaked out, screamed, and left.

Mickey sat back on the couch pretty proud of his machete throw, and then he promptly passed out. He said the next thing he knew, he was being shaken awake by a cop. His wife had called the law. Mickey was arrested wearing nothing but his underwear through the whole thing. Mickey said he remembered mainly two things about being arrested. One, they wouldn't let him put on any more clothes. And two, the cops weren't impressed with the perfectly thrown machete sticking in the wall. He had asked.

Once, years ago, I told this story to one of my best friends, Rich Porter, who was an attorney in Atlanta at the time. One day he called me and said that a fellow attorney was quitting the practice and was moving to Nashville to try to make it as songwriter and singer. He said his friend wanted to talk to me about the Mickey canned good story. He thought there might be a song there.

I don't listen to a lot of country music, so I'm not sure if the song ever got written or if it received any airtime. I doubt it has. I always thought this was a humorous story about reaching one's breaking point. Take my TV, my stereo, my bank account, but, by God, you don't have to take my canned goods, too, do you?

I often wonder what my own breaking point may be.

FIRST IMPRESSIONS

Now my friend Sammy told me this story, shortly after it happened. He's my friend whose stepfather and coworker had shot up the canned goods. Some time had passed since then, and in this story, Sammy was no longer living with his mom and stepfather in Chuluota. He and a roommate were living in an apartment closer to Orlando.

I remember stopping by there one time with a friend. It was a downstairs apartment in a two-story apartment complex. Their living room had a big set of sliding glass doors looking out onto a small patio. When my friend and I stopped by, Sammy and his roommate were getting ready to go out for the evening. They were probably hitting a couple of bars. His roommate, who we had just met, was talking to us, and casually strapped a small pistol on to his ankle under his pants leg. This would have been around 1980. Not very many people were carrying guns back then. I thought it was unusual, but not over the top. But then he pulled up his other pant leg, and I noticed that ankle was shaved. He then proceeded to tape extra bullets to that leg. He was doing all of this without discussing it. He just kept on with the conversation all the while arming his self for a night out on the town. Nothing going on here. At the time, I thought I could possibly understand why someone would carry a hidden gun, but extra bullets? Maybe he was concerned with possibly getting pinned down. I just met him, so I didn't ask. This is just my remembrance of the one and only time I met Sammy's roommate. Some of us Chuluota people did seem to attract some different type people into our lives. Hell, Sammy's stepdad's friend helped shoot up the canned goods in the kitchen. Maybe it ran in their family.

I ran into Sammy a few weeks after stopping by his apartment and meeting his roommate for the first time. We were just doing the usual small talk when Sammy mentioned he was in the process of moving out of his apartment. Of course, I asked why. He said there had been an incident.

Sammy and his roommate were going out on a double date one night. Sammy was with his girlfriend and his roommate was on a first date with a woman, who had come to Sammy's apartment. They were all sitting in the living room discussing plans for the upcoming evening. Suddenly the front door crashed in. Cops streamed in, guns drawn, screaming, "No one move, police!"

Sammy said they were all very startled, as one could imagine, their brains trying to compute what the hell was happening. He said that the second cop, who ran in the apartment, stumbled, and his shot gun accidentally went off and blew out the sliding glass doors. The two girls screamed, and the roommate's date instantly peed her pants. Sammy said it was pure chaos for a few minutes.

According to Sammy, the cops had the wrong apartment. No one was arrested. No one sued anyone—times were different back then. Sammy said the roommate's date was scared and embarrassed for peeing her pants. She managed to pull herself together enough to leave, never to be heard from again. Imagine that. I know at the time it was very scary and not funny. But now, years later, it strikes me as funny. Could you imagine that being your first date? From either perspective, the girl's or the guy's. The girl would always wonder, "who are these guys, and was it really the wrong place?" The guy, if really interested in the girl, would know there is no chance for making this up. I bet the girl did repeat the story many times in her life though.

Sammy said that because no one was arrested, the apartment manager believed Sammy that the cops just had the wrong place. They replaced the sliding glass doors, but asked Sammy and his roommate to move out anyway because the neighbors no longer felt comfortable around them. Imagine that. Some first impression on that first date.

THE BURNING

This story is probably one of the prouder memories I have of the group of Chuluota people we referred to as the younger generation. They were several years younger than us, so we didn't hang with them much, but we all knew one another.

Pat Rodgers was one of this generation, and I referred to him as my boy or son, although he was only four or five years younger. Everyone liked Pat, myself included. He was a good-looking kid. He looked like a surfer with bleached blonde hair who had just blown in off the beach. I had the surfer look going, too, but I don't think my hair was as blonde as Pat's. Because of similar looks, but mainly because I would be proud to be associated with Pat, I referred to him as my son. Pat always seemed to be in a good mood and laughing. Again, everyone liked him. Tragically, he was killed in an accident while in his early twenties. I mention Pat because I believe he was the mastermind behind this story. Another proud moment of Chuluota lore.

I got home from work one day, and I got a phone call from someone telling me to turn on my TV. There on the local news was a story unfolding of the county police raiding a large patch of pot growing in the nearby woods. The wooded area was behind an orange grove, which was just behind First Street in Chuluota. A helicopter was involved—I think it's how they spotted the pot—as well as a bunch of police and vehicles. Also, quite a few town people had gathered on First Street to watch the goings on. Quite the circus.

The plants were fairly large and numbered in the hundreds. It was enough plants that the police decided to pull them up, pile them, and burn them right there on the spot, as opposed to hauling them off. I remember watching this on TV and wondering whose plants they were. I was really surprised that I didn't know. In fact, as far as I know, we never did find out. This is hard to pull off in a small town.

Finally, the show was over. The news crews left, the helicopter flew off, the cops drove away, and the people on First Street went back home.

Pat—who I'm giving full credit for this brilliant idea—said, "Hmm."

He and a couple of his friends went out behind First Street and promptly put the fire out. I believe they rescued about six pounds of unburned pot. Some smelled and tasted like diesel fuel, but not too much. Another proud Chuluota moment. These boys were all of fifteen years old.

THE CHARLIE CHIPS CAN

From the age of four to twelve, I lived in the woods about a mile out of Chuluota. Our closest neighbors were the Johnsons. They lived about a mile away. Mr. and Mrs. Johnson had two adopted sons, Brian and Josh. Brian was nine months older than me, and Josh was a couple of years younger. It was obvious they were from different biological parents. Josh was pretty much a constant. A fairly good kid, and later on, a good adult. Now Brian was a different story. He had some great mechanical abilities. He could be smart, polite, and kind. However, he could also be mean, crazy, and disrespectful. He would probably be diagnosed nowadays as bipolar. Brian hung out with us quite a bit on weekends and during the summer.

The parents, Mr. and Mrs. Johnson, were older when they adopted. They were always nice and very good to me. It was Mr. Johnson who had originally gotten me somewhat focused on bottle hunting. He liked exploring and looking for things. He was the first person I knew who had a metal detector. He had the great talent of telling a story and passing on the excitement he felt. He was also a rarity in that he had been born and raised in Orlando. He had gone to school with Buddy Epson—Jed Clampett from *Beverly Hillbillies* TV fame. I remember Mr.

Johnson telling me his first driver's license was on a piece of paper that the chief of police of Orlando had written these words, "I hereby certify that Ted Johnson can drive." He was twelve years old at the time.

I always liked the Johnsons. I felt bad about how Brian treated them at times. He got picked on and beat up by some of his peers, probably indirectly for being disrespectful and mean to his parents. Hard to be in a screwed-up home life and watch a peer cussing and disrespecting their parents who we deemed were good. We were wishing we could trade places. I could whip Brian in a fight if I could keep him from getting me on the ground because he was bigger than me. We didn't fight too many times.

This story is of one of the many crazy things I saw Brian do while we were quite young. Someone had shown my brother, Larry, what they thought was a neat trick. So, he showed us, too. My brother took a metal coffee can, one that came with a plastic lid, and he took a nail and a hammer and punched a hole in the side of the can just above the bottom. He then put a couple of drops of gasoline in the can and put the plastic lid back on. He then lit a candle and held the candle under the can moving it back and forth for a few seconds, thus turning the few drops of gas into a vapor. He then put the candle out, set the can down, and lit a match and stuck it in the hole in the bottom side. This resulted in there being a pretty loud *voorump, and* the lid blew ten to fifteen feet in the air. We thought this was kind of a cool trick and repeated it a few times.

A few days later, Larry and I walked to the Johnsons house in the evening. We sometimes went and got Brian and went for long walks in the evening. Lots of times, we wore headlamps to shine on critters that came out at night. It was probably five or six in the summer evening when we got to their house this one time, and it was still light out.

We went up on the little porch of their house and knocked on the door and Mr. Johnson answered. We asked for Brian. He told us he hadn't seen Brian in a while and wasn't sure where he was. Then from the porch he spotted Brian.

"There he is in the orange grove doing something," he said.

We could see Brian on his knees busy with something.

Brian knew we were coming over and was going to surprise us. Unbeknownst to us, Brian had decided to try the trick Larry had shown us. In Brian's mind, bigger is better. It's not entirely Brian's fault for thinking this way. Lots of guys do. It probably has something to do with women telling us this for one hundred thousand plus years. Anyway, Brian decided to use a Charlie Chips can instead of a coffee can. For those who don't know, there was a truck much like the old milk trucks that would come around and deliver potato chips and pretzels. My family didn't partake in this service, but the Johnsons did. The can the chips came in was approximately sixteen inches across and about sixteen inches deep with a metal lid that pressed down into place. Brian had taken the can and punched a hole in the side near the bottom—so much for the refund deposit on the can—and had poured about a quarter inch of gasoline in the can. He put the lid back on and ran a lit candle under the bottom for a few seconds—enough time to let some of the gas vaporize, but not all of it. Brian was now trying to light it, but his matches kept going out. I suspect because of too much liquid. We were wondering what he was doing when on about his third attempt it lit. There was a loud bang and a roar as the lid was blown over a hundred feet in the air. It was spinning and on fire. Brian was instantly knocked off his knees and onto his back. He was scared but unhurt. He was probably around ten years old at the time. Possibly a little older but not much, if any.

I remember that Larry, Mr. Johnson, and I were taking it all in and our heads were all turned upward watching the spinning, burning metal lid. Mr. Johnson, and most adults of the time, tried not to cuss too much around kids. But I still can remember him calmly and quietly saying, "son of a bitch."

Then the burning, spinning metal lid that was on fire landed. Because it was spinning at a high rate of speed, when it hit, it took off rolling across the ground leaving a trail of fire as it went. This was now catching the grass in the orange grove on fire. Mr. Johnson was no longer caring about cussing in front of kids. He was screaming something like, "Son of a bitch. Have you lost your mind?" as he ran towards Brian probably wanting to kill him. Brian now alerted to the real danger, began to run.

For the most part, Brian could outrun his parents and would stay out of reach until they calmed down. Sometimes it took hours or longer. Larry and I were the ones who put the fire out while Mr. Johnson chased after Brian. I feel quite confident that, in the history of man, never has a Charlie Chip can ever been used in this way. Bigger, better? Definitely crazier, and more impressive than the original trick using a mere coffee can.

FIRST CARS

The previous story about Brian Johnson made me think of first cars, his and mine. Brian had been driving something since he was a small kid. It's a wonder he never killed his younger brother, Josh. He started with a Gravely riding lawn mower. He moved up to a full-size tractor at a young age. Then his family got a tractor with a large bucket on the front end. Brian was driving this by the age of ten. I remember seeing Brian dump a whole front bucket load of dirt onto a friend of ours. This friend would probably have killed Brian, but Brian had driven a long way away by the time the kid got dug out. Also, I saw Brian talk his little brother into getting into the bucket so he could lift him up and down. All fun, until Brian raised the bucket as far as it would go and started driving down the road as fast as it would go. Josh was hanging on for dear life in the bucket, which was at least eight feet off the ground. The tractor was going nearly thirty miles an hour down the road with Josh cussing and spitting at Brian. Brian just laughed. Josh survived.

I walked to the Johnson's house one afternoon, and when I approached, Brian suddenly drove his grandfather's car out of the orange grove. His grandfather had come to live with them for a little while. He passed away shortly after doing so. So, the grandfather was dead by the time Brian did this, and there were no adults at home. It was only natural that Brian would fire up the car. It was a cool car—a 1942 Pontiac with running boards on the side. Brian had put a few boards down on the front seat and piled a couple of pillows on top of those so he could see over the high dashboard. Brian was about ten when he slid sideways out of the orange grove in the way-cool old car and onto the old gravel road that ran in front of their house. One way or another, the parents must have found out. Cool car got sold shortly after Brian's driving adventure.

Anyway, I remember Brian's first car was a 1960-something Ford station wagon. It had no reverse gear, or at least one that worked. He had to put some thought into where he parked it. There was lots of getting out and pushing at times. One time, Brian had gotten a free car wash for something. Probably buying a certain amount of gas at a gas station. We had just pulled into the car wash, and it had started spraying water, and for some reason, the attendant wanted us to back up. Of course, we couldn't with no reverse. The attendant ended up getting in the running car wash and pushing us backwards. He got wet and a little beat up by the spinning rag things. He wasn't happy.

It was in this car where Brian happened to leave a car inner tube and a long rope. They had been water skiing earlier in the day and pulling this inner tube behind the boat. This discovery of the inner tube and rope was the beginning of a sport we invented that ended up morphing into what became known as dooring, but that will be told in another story.

Brian got his car when he was sixteen. I had to wait until I could buy my own. I was eighteen and had already graduated high school. These first cars that my friends and I owned would in this day—and probably were at the time by adults—be deemed pieces of junk. We, however, thought of them as having character. We may have been grasping at straws with that outlook, but at least we were no longer walking or hitchhiking. Not to mention us being poor, it was the best we could do.

My first car was a 1962 Buick LaSabre. It had a 410-wild cat motor in it and got about eight miles to the gallon. The whole car had been painted with a paint brush. The man I bought it from lived on the highway that went into Chuluota. He sold honey and sometimes cars. He wanted two hundred and fifty dollars for it. I talked him down to two hundred thirty-five because it had a busted headlight and a bad exhaust leak. The exhaust wasn't connected to the manifold, and it was real loud. I was a shrewd negotiator.

This car had been a large luxury car in its day in 1962. Not so much in 1977. It was huge. We could sit four people up front and four in the back and not touch one another. It had all kinds of lights in the car in different locations. They were called courtesy lights. They came in handy for rolling joints anywhere in the car at night. A real courtesy.

On the day I bought it, I drove over to my friend Robert Osbourne's house. He was, and is, better known simply as Oz by most. He was still living at his mom's house with his stepdad in Chuluota. When I pulled into the driveway his stepdad came out, looked around, then went back inside. A moment later, Oz came outside laughing. I asked him what was so funny. He said his stepdad had come outside because he thought a helicopter was landing in the street. The car was that loud. I got it fixed fairly quickly. One never wanted to draw the attention of the cops more than the long hair and other traits already did.

Often times, I would find Oz or someone else sleeping in the back seat of my car in the mornings. People knew that the back seat was about the same size as a single bed and comfortable. If they had a night of partying and couldn't, or didn't want to, go home, they'd simply crawl into my back seat and go to sleep. I never locked it.

I ran into my cousin's husband, Leon, one day. He asked me what was wrong with my car. I asked him what he meant.

"Well, I saw it parked on the side of the highway the other day, and a few days before that, I saw it beside Second Street. And about two weeks ago, I saw it beside Sixth Street."

I told him that there wasn't anything wrong with it, I just kept running out of gas.

"What? Your gas gauge doesn't work?"

I told him it worked fine, there was just nothing I could do about it. Gas was cheap, but when you're not making much money and only getting eight miles to a gallon, well …

I didn't have that car too long. Two friends and I had flown to Houston, Texas, to join two other friends who were already out there. Houston was booming. The want ads sections were as big as the entire *Orlando Sentinel* newspaper. We flew out, and I left the car behind at my mother's. When I came back in about two months, my car was gone. My off-the-wall stepdad took it one night and had gotten a DUI arrest while driving it. The police impounded the car. I called to see how much they wanted to get it out. They wanted more than I had paid for the car for towing and storage. I had no choice but to let them keep it. The car deserved a better ending. But, I guess, most of my early cars deserved better endings. Several I wrecked.

SCREWING ONE AROUND

For some reason, I have had some trouble starting this story. I've started it several times. Each time I stumble over trying to explain why acts like this were done. Looking back, the characters seem kind of mean. But the guys in this story were not acting out of meanness. They saw this as an opportunity to screw around with one of their friends. They fully expected they would be screwed around with similarly if the opportunity presented itself. They would be correct in thinking this way. There was a lot of screwing each other around, but, thankfully, mostly in high school. This story takes place in Mr. Meckler's eleventh grade history class. To me, there was talent involved. The two guys doing the screwing around did some good straight-faced acting.

Most of our classes in high school had different levels of students in them. Some kids were going to college, and some were not going to graduate high school. A classroom of smart kids, dumb kids, and more. In fact, the only classes I know where an effort was made to separate students by their progress was the math classes. Mr. Meckler was an elderly man who just didn't really understand my generation. I believe he may have been too old to have been in World War II. He was older than my parents, who had lived through the Great War. I do remember he had been in the service, though, because he could kill a whole class hour telling us the proper way to dig a fox hole.

My good friend Rich Porter was in this class. I have known Rich since the first grade. He lived briefly on the same street as my grandmother in Chuluota. This is how I first met him. His family moved to the outskirts of Chuluota early on, though. I hunted and fished and did other things with him as a kid. But for the most part, we didn't hang out too much in high school. Rich was smart and was going to college. He didn't hang out with me and my peers running the streets of Chuluota. Smart move. Rich was a good-looking guy and a good student. Everyone liked Rich—girls, teachers, and everyone else. Robert Osbourne (Oz) and Slim Richardson liked Rich, too. They just saw an opportunity one day to screw him around.

On this particular day, Rich had a rather large zit on his nose. I'm sure, we can all remember how important looks and image are in high school. So, a zit can be a fairly big deal to a teenager, especially in an obvious place. You just have to do the best you can for a few days until it passes. Rich was doing this, I'm sure, while trying to keep a somewhat low profile sitting in his desk.

Oz came strolling into class just before the bell rang. His route to get to his desk took him past Rich at his desk. When Oz passed, he noticed Rich's zit on his nose.

"Good Lord, what the hell is that?" Oz said in his loudest voice.

"Go to hell, Oz, and go sit down," Rich growled.

Oz pretended he never even heard Rich. He just put his hands on his hips and bent way over with his face real close to Rich's, staring intently at Rich's nose. He moved side to side to get a better angle.

"Damn," he'd say or "good Lord."

Rich was getting a little embarrassed and told Oz to go sit the hell down. Oz, of course, didn't pay any attention and called Slim Richardson over to come look.

"Slim, come look at this," Oz said.

Slim walked over. "What's up?"

"What the hell is wrong with Rich's face?" Oz pointed to Rich's nose. "Look at that big thing on Rich's nose. What the hell is that?"

Slim bent over and got real close to Rich's face. Oz leaned, too. Rich became more embarrassed and told them both to get screwed and to go sit the hell down. They acted like they never heard Rich.

"I think it's a big zit," Slim said.

"Oh no, no, no." Oz leaned closer. "That's way too big for a zit. That's got to be something like a spider bite."

Slim chuckled, while a few others, who were watching, laughed.

"A spider bite?" Slim asked.

"Yeah, I've seen zits, and that is way too big for a zit. Got to be like a spider bite. Count, come look at this."

Dennis Countly we knew from school. They called him Count for short. He was mostly into being cool, dressing nice, and trying to impress the girls. Count walked over. Oz told him to look at Rich's nose. Rich was now about to die. Mr. Meckler finally came over and interceded.

"Okay, boys, let's all have a seat. We're going to have a quiz today."

"As a friend, I'm telling you, you need to have that looked at," Count said to Rich on his way to his seat.

We were all in our seats now, but Oz and Slim kept getting about half way up in their seats and kept looking back towards Rich, moving their heads from side to side and up and down to get a better angle. Sometimes making "tsk tsk" noises.

"There are ten questions on the quiz today," Mr. Meckler said. We were supposed to have read material for homework. "The first five are multiple choice, and the other five are short essay questions. Are there any questions before I hand out the quiz?"

Slim immediately raised his hand, and Mr. Meckler rolled his eyes.

"Yes, Slim, what is it?"

"Does Rich have to take the quiz?" Slim asked. "He has a big ole spider bite on his nose."

Quite a bit of laughter erupted in the room. Rich, about to die, realized just in case, by some miracle, someone in the back of the room didn't know he had a big zit on his nose, they now knew.

"Yes, Slim, Mr. Porter will be taking the quiz. You need to be more concerned about your own results because you're not doing too well in here."

"Mr. Meckler, that's not right," Slim said. "How's Rich going to concentrate on taking a quiz when he has a big ole spider bite on his nose?"

"Yes, Mr. Meckler, I think I may have to side with Slim and Oz on this one," Count said. "I think you may have it wrong."

Rich slid further down in his desk. I'm sure he felt like melting into the floor.

The quiz went on. Rich survived. Rich went on to be a successful attorney and is, one of, if not my best friend, to this day. Rich tells me that one thing he remembers about this class was that he was trying to make good grades, and these guys could have cared less. That was them. They didn't care about the class or school in general. They were there for sports, and mainly, for the social life.

I would like to take the opportunity to add, later in the year, in the same class, Meckler sent Oz to the office for farting. That was the only time I have ever heard of this happening to anyone. To this day, Oz is the only person I have known who could fart on command. There is no doubt in my mind if someone needed to, they could wake up Oz in the middle of the night and ask him to fart, and he could do it. He once told me with a straight face that some people could draw and paint and some could sing, but he could fart. It was his gift from God. They were also pretty rank for added bonus. But I don't want to talk too much about that kind of thing. It kind of seems like cheap bathroom humor, but I did think it was worth mentioning because he got sent to the office for it.

"The Constitution of the United States gives me the right to expect clean air," Mr. Meckler announced as he sent Oz packing. "And, as far as I'm concerned, Mr. Osbourne, you can go out to the Port-a-Potty on the baseball field and rot."

Oz tried to convince Mr. Meckler that he was really embarrassed by it. "I got a physical kidney problem."

Mr. Meckler wasn't buying it. Rightfully so. We usually got paddled for the stupid stuff we did when we got sent to the office. I don't think Oz got paddled this time. He may have straight-faced convinced them he had a kidney problem. Anyway, Oz is the only person I ever heard of getting sent to the office for farting. To this day, it is one of Oz's proudest moments. This is just another example of what I have always thought of as a common, somewhat twisted, pride thing shared by many of my fellow Chuluotians. Oz was a very talented athlete. He was good at both football and baseball. He alone was responsible for his baseball team to have won several games. However, I never once heard him brag or boast on any of those achievements. Now, him getting kicked out of class and sent to the office for farting, I have heard him mention and brag on that several times, along with a few other farting stories.

A FEW MORE OZ STORIES

Oz was and is one of a kind. That is an understatement for sure. Oz, for the most part, never took himself or anyone, for that matter, very seriously. Not taking much seriously or caring what others think can lead to some interesting actions.

I first met Oz when I was ten or eleven. His family had moved near Rich Porter's house on the outskirts of Chuluota. I met him there. My parents and his divorced near the same time. I had moved into Chuluota with my mother and soon-to-be stepdad. Oz moved into Chuluota with his mom and two brothers. One older brother, one younger brother. We started hanging out together.

One of the first memories I have of Oz is when I went to the house they were living in when they first moved into Chuluota. I knocked on the door, and Oz yelled for me to come in. When I walked in, he was mopping the ceiling in the kitchen. I asked him what the hell he was doing.

"Help me clean this up before someone comes home."

"What the hell happened?" I asked.

"I was heating up a can of chili on the stove."

"Damn, didn't you open it first?"

"No."

We were about twelve at the time, but I knew better than that. Apparently, Oz didn't. It appeared to be a rather violent explosion. Luckily, he didn't get killed. I'm not sure if his mom ever found out. I wouldn't be surprised if she did because there was chili everywhere.

Now a lot of girls liked Oz. He had dirty blondish hair and was a good athlete. He excelled in baseball and football and played both in high school. My brother never understood why I liked Oz and hung around him because Oz could be quite nasty and didn't mind embarrassing me in front of people. All of this is true, and I never did like it. But I understood in Oz's mind he didn't mean any harm. He expected people to screw him around in return, and he would have been okay with it. I really don't remember anyone screwing Oz around though, besides his older brother and his brother's best friend, Johnny McCallister. I knew that while Oz was capable of screwing me around and did, he was also loyal and honest. I remember when I was around thirteen, I had gotten my foot hurt pretty bad. The doctors told me to stay off my feet for a month. But at thirteen, I was afraid I might miss something, and coupled with hating my home life, I was hobbling out the door on crutches in about a week and a half. But for that first week and a half, while I was confined mostly to my couch, Oz came and saw me every day. He would bring me a Pepsi and some kind of pastry from the local store. This was a big deal to me for us kids didn't have much money at all. So, spending quite a bit of what he had meant a lot. Also, to this day, Oz is the only one from the old Chuluota gang I ran with who makes an effort to stay in touch. When I first moved away, for several years, I called others and would send Christmas cards, and tried to stay in touch from afar. They'd talk to me if I got them on the phone. But they never made an effort to write or call me on their own. So, after a few years, I quit making the effort to stay in contact with them. All but Oz. We still talk at least once a month, although he lives quite some ways away.

In high school, Oz dated this nice, good looking, fairly innocent girl who was a cheerleader and lived in another town. For the most part, he kept his twisted Chuluota-self hidden from her. Smart move. He was going to take her to homecoming or the prom, I don't remember now. He decided to get his hair permed in somewhat of an Afro style for the event. It was an accepted style, though most people I knew wouldn't do it. All long hair of any kind was in style, though. For some reason, the hair place couldn't finish Oz's hair that day. They only did half the treatment and told him to come back. I think they screwed up and knew it. Anyway, Oz never went back. End result was this large dirty blonde poof of hair on top of his head. He found out that if he tried to comb it, the hair would come out in large amounts. I think they must have burned it chemically. So, Oz just decided to quit combing it. He told me he set it free.

"Me and Breyer's Ice Cream have gone back to nature," he said.

Much to my amazement, women seemed to like the look. I said it made him look like a Dr. Seuss Who person from the *How the Grinch Stole Christmas* fame. I—and some others—called him Who for short sometimes. But most called him Oz. Sometimes people called him Robert, or even Turtle, which was his Dad's name for him. But not many.

On occasion, Oz would Afro his hair with an Afro hair pick. It would really poof up. I noticed that when he did this, it seemed to put his hair on a half of a second delay. He could walk up, and when he stopped, his hair seemed to take a half of a second to catch up. It would come forward past his face and rock back and forth a time or two and then stop. Or, if he turned his head quickly to the side, it seemed to take a half second for his hair to respond and turn, too. Half a second hair delay, an interesting thing. Oz liked the effect, and he used it.

Oz and I used to fish quite a bit together. We were both pretty good at bass fishing. One of the great things about Chuluota was that I had at least thirty different places to bass fish. Everything from large lakes to very small ponds and all sizes in between. Often the small ponds weren't known to others and were hard to get to. I had a few, I was certain, where I was the only one fishing them. Anyway, one afternoon, Oz and I were fishing on a small out of the way pond I had recently found out about. We were fishing out of a canoe. Not sure now where the canoe came from. I usually had a small Jon boat, or we would wade fish. I hadn't fished out of a canoe very often and Oz even less.

I gave Oz at least a five-minute lecture on how we needed to be careful not to flip the canoe over. It's easy to do, especially while moving around fishing. This also was a remote, somewhat alligator- and snake-infested looking pond. We had caught three or four bass and had them tied to the canoe on a stringer. I'm sure we had been drinking beer and probably experimenting with marijuana. It's what we did. I stood up in the canoe to pee over the side, explaining to Oz how we had to be careful.

At this point, I'll take responsibility for losing my balance and feeling like the canoe was going to flip over. As the unbalancing began, I remember thinking, *if I go ahead and jump overboard, perhaps I can keep the canoe and Oz from flipping over.* In what I thought was a heroic and noble fashion, I went ahead and jumped in the spooky-looking pond. I remember that as soon as I hit and went under the surface, I immediately came back up to see if indeed my heroic action had saved the canoe and Oz from flipping over. As I cleared the surface, I saw the canoe on its side, then Oz's head broke the surface about four feet from me. He had this big ole wet glob of hair on his head, not near as poofy as usual. He gave me this disgusted look and was about to say something, when all of a sudden, the fish on the stringer wrapped around his leg, and he screamed. The combination of the wet Who-person look and the screaming from the fish being wrapped around his leg in this spooky-looking pond just hit me as very funny. Still does. Oz, I don't think, could get mad at me, because I was laughing so hard.

I don't remember all the details anymore, but I don't think we lost any fishing equipment. It was a fairly shallow pond. I know we saved the canoe and the fish. I just remember the wet Who-looking person, screaming with the fish—that were attempting to swim away— wrapped around his leg. All after I had given a long canoe safety lecture.

This next story takes place in a Krystal hamburger place. At this time, this was the only place in the area that stayed open late that sold food. They stayed open until one o'clock in the morning. They sold hamburgers, French fries and soft drinks. It was around fifteen miles out of Chuluota, in an area called Casselberry. The poor people who worked there probably saw just about everything there was to see late at night. We were now eighteen and were more mobile with more of us owning cars. Sometimes, we'd go towards the end of a night of partying to get something to eat. Many other young people from nearby towns and areas were doing the same thing. Lots of the people were coming from bars and such. We may have been, too. I don't remember now. I do remember we all had a good buzz on, and we were hungry.

There were four of us. Oz, Slim Richardson, Jim Hicks, and myself. Just before we walked in, without saying a word, Oz pulled his pants down just as low as they would go without falling off. This was about thirty years before the look was popular. Now Oz didn't wear underwear. So, the end result was the bottom of his shirt was about on his hips and the top of his pants was resting on the beginning of his penis. Most of his pubic hair was exposed along with part of his ass in the rear. We thought it was kind of comical as we all walked in.

We got in line to place our orders with the people working behind the counter. I think Jim was first in line in our group, then Oz, Slim, and myself. There were others in line and more coming in. I was checking out people's reaction when they saw Oz. He was straight faced, being serious, just like it was another day. The people behind the counter were trying not to look and laugh as they took Oz's order. Oz was dead serious—*nothing going on here*—as he made his order. We made our orders to eat there, as opposed to getting food to go. In a few minutes, Oz got his food on a tray and started to walk towards the tables.

When Oz began to walk away from the counter with a tray full of food in his hands, Slim, who was already behind him, reached out and pulled his pants down. It didn't take much of a tug to do this. Oz now had a tray full of food in his hands, and his pants around his ankles.

He stood naked from the waist down in the middle of the restaurant. People were laughing. Oz didn't panic or smile, he just proceeded to take little shuffling steps, with his pants around his ankles and carrying his tray, towards a table. Oz was doing a good job of staying composed and straight faced while he took his little steps. About this time, four young black girls walked in. They were laughing and in mid-animated conversation, when one of them spotted Oz who now was only about ten feet from them. The black girl stopped everything and pointed at Oz and said real loud, "Woo a woo, that white boy ain't got no clothes on, swear to God."

They all fell out, and so did we, along with many others in the restaurant. This proved a little too much even for Oz. He started laughing and ended up yanking his pants back up pretty quick. Other than that, the meal was uneventful.

Another time, Slim and Jim had Oz with them. They were all going out to a bar or two that night. On the way, they stopped at these girls' apartment. Slim and Jim had met them a few weeks earlier at a bar. They didn't know them well, just stopped by to see if they were home. Maybe to smoke a joint. Two of the three girls who lived there were home and invited them in. Slim and Jim introduced Oz to them. The girls greeted them and told them to make themselves at home. Oz almost immediately went into their bathroom, took his clothes off and came back out buck naked. He acted like he was real messed up—either drunk or on drugs—for a short time, and then just pretended to pass out on their couch. Slim and Jim kind of smiled and chuckled, but they weren't overly surprised. Once you got to know Oz, you soon realized you weren't too surprised by anything he did. The girls were surprised, a little stunned, and asked why Oz was now naked and passed out on their couch. Slim and Jim told them mainly because the girls had told him to make himself at home. One of the girls placed a towel over Oz's lap as he proceeded to pretend he was passed out.

Shortly afterward, the third roommate came home. She said hello to Slim and Jim and then noticed Oz on the couch. She asked her roommates why there was a guy on their couch with a towel on his lap.

They told her they merely had told him to make his self at home, and he had come out of the bathroom naked.

"No!" she yelled and lifted up one end of the towel to look underneath. "I'll be damned."

Oz told me later he thought this was damn humorous.

Soon it was time to leave and go to the bar. They said their goodbyes and gently shook Oz to wake him from his pretend pass out. He got up, put his clothes back on, said it was nice to meet them, and they left. I asked Oz why he did this after hearing the story.

"Ah, it seemed like the thing to do." His world was different than most.

Another time Oz, Slim, Jim, and myself were up at the ABC bar. It was real popular at the time and had a round bar in it that revolved. It was on the outskirts of Orlando and Altamonte in the area called Casselberry. Lots of women went to this bar. All the women made it popular. Also, disco had just come out, and this was the kind of music that was played there. I didn't like the music, but there were women, and it was something to do on the weekend. So sometimes I went. I liked going with Oz because he was like me, in that he went just to have a good time and laugh. It wasn't a big deal to try to pick up women. Slim and Jim were more into being cool and trying to pick up women. Jim and Slim had mostly a humorous and twisted side to them. It's the reason we spent time with one another. Just in this particular phase, they were trying to dress nice, be cool, and pick up women. This bar was big enough and crowded enough that it was easy to get separated and not see the people you came with for periods of time. One particular night, Oz was real drunk early on, and I hadn't seen him in a while. He'd already done some pretty crazy things. About this time, Slim came up to me.

"Come check this out, this is going to be good," he said.

Oz was heading out onto the dance floor with some girl. The poor girl must have just gotten to the bar, and hadn't seen Oz, and didn't know how drunk he was. Like I said earlier, lots of girls thought Oz was good looking. The dance floor was big but always very packed. Oz and the girl proceeded to dance, as Slim and I watched waiting for Oz to do something crazy. Well, Oz danced seriously for about five seconds. Then he placed his hands over his face and proceeded to run in place as fast as he could. The girl tried pulling Oz's hands away from his face, but Oz kept putting them back and running in place. All of a sudden, Oz just dropped to the dance floor and began rolling around as fast as he could. He was rolling into people, tripping people up, and people were trying to get out of his way. The girl had eased off the dance floor by now, I'm sure wondering, what the hell was that? Oz suddenly stopped rolling around, and while still on the floor and now sitting, he crossed his legs and held his arms straight out in front of himself and began chanting "om" real loud. People didn't understand, but they were laughing.

We were laughing along with all the others. Oz staggered off the dance floor, I think feeling better about himself, having gotten that out of his system. Looking back, this may be what the snooty people who are trained in dance would refer to as primitive interpretive dance. Or perhaps not.

PENIS STORIES

Up to this point, I haven't told any stories about myself. I think perhaps I do better as an observer. Or maybe, I have suppressed stories of myself. Let the psychologists debate this. Two stories about myself do come to mind, and I shall tell them. Both involve my penis. For some reason, this seems appropriate. I defer to the psychologists once again. These stories seem funny now—the theme I'm trying to stay with—but I'm sure they weren't at the time.

Story one. In ninth grade, I decided to take an art class. I took it for no other reason than I thought it would be an easy class and an easy credit. It was. I had no talent in art and no great interest. Much to my surprise, there were only about fifteen people in the class—all girls, except me and two other guys. Not that this ratio ever did me any good in this class. Another huge bonus was the teacher was very good looking with long strawberry blonde hair. She was probably in her late twenties, and I think, of the hippie persuasion. She didn't always wear a bra, which again was an added plus. You have to remember this was around 1974, and this was very common dress at that time, and my school had a few very lax years. I also remember that the teacher had a boyfriend who sat in class from time to time. He had long hair and looked stoned to me. I know these things because I was very familiar with the condition by this time. He would spend most of the time staring at the high school girls.

Okay, that's a little background on my art teacher—Ms. Vickers, God bless her. Now, for a couple of weeks in this class, the students took turns modeling. We would stand or sit in a pose on top of a table. The rest of the students would sit around the table and draw the model.

When my turn came to model, I was posed standing on the table. I was wearing tight light blue pants with big bell bottoms and a silk screen print shirt. This was a common style of the time. After a few minutes of posing, Ms. Vickers began going around the table checking on everyone's drawings. From my elevated position, I quickly noticed I could see down Ms. Vickers's shirt as she bent over checking everyone's work. She wasn't wearing a bra. Life was good. I could see both breasts complete with nipples. Most of us guys know, it doesn't count unless you see nipple. This counted in a big way. Because of the common fashion of the time, I was on high alert to the fact of no bras and was always vigilant.

For a fifteen-year-old red-blooded American youth, I was in quite an envious position. Here I was seeing a beautiful, older woman's breast. Not only that, but I was at school. Furthering my education, I might add. Life was good. Now a huge drawback on being a red-blooded American fifteen-year-old male is this: it takes nothing at all to get an erection. One could get one from the mere mention of a breast, a change in wind direction, or for no reason at all. I began feeling movement in my light blue pants.

"Oh no," I thought.

I was wearing tight pants, and everyone was staring intensely at me while drawing. I'm moments away from growing—quite immensely I might add—and perhaps even throbbing. After all, I am fifteen. I could just imagine the girls giggling and pointing. Or worst, complaining to Ms. Vickers that Mark was moving, and now they were going to have to erase. Damn. I began to panic.

Here I was in a great envious position that us fifteen-year-old males dream about. I now had to look away and start thinking about cold things. Somehow, I managed to refocus without causing myself great embarrassment. Damn, what a squandered opportunity, but I saw no way around it. I managed to de-erectify myself before anyone noticed and had to erase and start redrawing. After all these years, I still remember. Scarred, I'm sure; and yet another study for the psychologists.

To this day, my Chuluota peers and I can't believe it when we hear on the news of a male teenager turning in a woman teacher for having sex with them. We do realize these times are much different, though. In our world, that male student would have been beaten into the earth's crust for doing such a thing. This is a fantasy my friends and I shared about any good looking older female teacher. To violate such a pure and genuine fantasy by turning in said teacher would have been unimaginable, deserving of a beating, flogging, or public stoning.

Penis story number two. Thankfully, I don't have too many penis stories. If I did, I'd worry. Anyway, there was a time I stayed with the McAllister family. This was in my very early adulthood after graduating high school when I had a few periods where I was homeless. I was homeless before it was popular, I tell people. I bounced around a couple of places, had a few places of my own, two of those where I couldn't afford electricity. I slept in a friend's truck and other places. The point is, when you're young and you no longer have a home you can go to, or want to go to, it's hard. You have to be able to hold a regular job that's good enough to buy a car, afford rent, electricity, water, gas, insurance, and all the other things required to hold down a job. I managed to do it, but it took a while, with some favors from people and a few hard times along the way. I had also tried to attend college, but soon went broke among other troubles.

Where was I? Yes, I'm living with the McCallister family. I'm around twenty years old. I first met the McCallisters when I was five years old. Chuluota, for a couple of years, had a little league baseball team. My brother played on it, and I was the bat boy, for I was too young to play. But they did let me play in a couple of games because I was better than

71

a couple of the older guys. Anyway, I met Steve and Johnny through baseball around that time in my life. Steve was nine months older than me and became one of my best friends. Johnny was a couple of years older. You may remember him from the carnivorous armadillo story. The McCallister family was large, and I spent a lot of time at their house when I was young. Mr. McCallister got shot and killed in a bar when I was in fourth grade. So, all of the McCallister kids were young when this happened. This led to some dysfunction in their upbringing as one might guess. The McCallister children, going from youngest to oldest, were Karen, Ethan, Rachel, Kaitlin, Frida, Steve, Johnny, and Nell. There was also Mrs. McCallister, live and in color.

A brief overlook. I was twenty and staying with the McCallister family on First Street in Chuluota. Three of the kids had moved out by that time—Johnny, Steve, and Frida. I had gotten a job with my cousin's husband, Leon. Leon was a nice guy who got me a couple of early jobs in commercial construction. I worked steady at least forty hours a week as a carpenter's apprentice. Leon would pick me up every morning, and I'd ride to work with him. He lived only over on Second Street, so it wasn't too much of a burden on him. I think I gave him gas money, too.

Now Leon was real serious about being on time and not missing days. This was a good early habit for me to get into for work. I remember I worked more than a year straight before I missed a day because I was sick. It was a large company and a lot of employees stayed with them for a pretty long time. I worked there for more than six years, which is pretty rare for construction companies and employees. But alas, I've gotten side tracked again.

Leon used to pick me up around six in the morning. For some reason, I overslept one day. This was not like me. Maybe I partied the previous night. I don't remember now. I could pull that off when I was young. But on this particular morning, I awoke to fifteen-year-old Ethan McCallister opening up the bedroom door and saying that Leon was there to go to work. Damn. I jumped out of bed and grabbed my blue jeans and yanked them on. No underwear involved. I pulled up my jeans and yanked the zipper up. Then I felt immense pain. I looked down. Somehow, I managed to run about an inch and a half of penis skin in the zipper. Yes, it's kind of interwoven in the zipper. It hurts bad, but I realized I had to unzip it to free myself. So, I slowly unzipped that zipper back down. Much more pain, but no freedom. The skin was just staying interwoven into the zipper. Now it's early in the morning, and I was in a cold sweat. I took the zipper back up. More pain, no freedom. Damn, I'm hurt, late, and not sure what to do. I had to sit on edge of bed because of the intense pain.

Ethan stuck his head in the door again and asked me what was taking so long because Leon was waiting. I told Ethan my penis was stuck in my zipper.

He laughed.

"My uncle did that and had to get fifteen stitches," Ethan said.

"Get the hell out of here," I yelled, which made him laugh even harder. Still laughing, he left, and I heard him telling his mom and Leon what was going on. Laughing the whole time, I might add. Fifteen-year-olds can be cruel. I probably would have acted similar though. Then I heard them all laughing.

Mrs. McCallister came back to my room. She told me this is a common occurrence among little boys and can be easily remedied. Apparently, little boys sometimes get there little wee wees slightly caught in zippers, and it can be easily removed. This particular zipper was moving at a high rate of speed when it rolled over and took in an inch and a half of skin. I may have gone back down with the zipper in her presence to show the extent of the problem. I do remember, through the bouts of pain, flashing on old western movies, where the hero pulled the arrow out of himself that an Indian had shot him with. I told her to have Leon get me one of our razor knives out of our work aprons, which were in Leon's van. I was in immense pain. I was going to cut something.

A few minutes later, Leon reached through the doorway with a razor knife. Leon was old school and didn't want to see another man's penis, wounded or not. With the razor knife in hand, I contemplated cutting the zipper-caught penis skin off…for perhaps a half second. I soon came to my senses.

"Oh, hell no!" I thought. And then I proceeded to cut off my jeans.

I figured that if I could cut the zipper apart from the bottom perhaps I could separate it. This is what I did. I very carefully cut across one pant leg to the crotch area. During the process, Ethan would pop in and tell me about the uncle who had gotten fifteen stitches. Also, other people would come to the door, laughing, to get an update. I'm glad to say that my plan did work. Once I was able to cut over to the crotch area and cut away the zipper, I was able to separate it from the bottom. I was free. It was no easy task though. Levi's were well made. It was a pretty hard financial hit, too, for a dirt-poor youth to ruin a good pair of jeans. But, damn, I was free, and quite awake I might add, no coffee needed. Perhaps the most awake I have ever been.

Now I could end the story right there, but I feel I should tell one more thing. As mentioned earlier, Leon was a real stickler about being on time and not missing days of work. When Leon realized we were going to be a little late to work, he called the job. I'm not sure who he talked to or what he said. At the time, we were building a twelve-story office building in downtown Orlando and were pretty far along in its construction. Our company had a large crew on site with many other tradespeople. I would like to believe I was fairly well liked by our crew and the other trades people who knew me.

When we finally pulled up on the job site after my escape from my jeans, and I stepped out of the van, I heard cheering, clapping and, yes, laughter. People from the ground all the way up various levels of the mostly skeletal building were letting me know that word had traveled, and they knew of my morning ordeal. I believed I bowed and informed them that anyone who wished to kiss my wound and make it feel better could form a line. After all, I was a tough construction worker.

Sometime during that day, I had to go to the job trailer, which served as our office. A young female secretary put her hand on my shoulder and asked if I was okay. It took me a brief moment to realize she was sincere, for no one else had been concerned about my health.

They were tough construction workers, and this was another man's penis. I thanked her for her concern. I was touched and also aroused. I might have been a tough construction worker, but I was young and easily aroused.

Earlier, I wrote I was thankful I didn't have many penis stories. Well, I'm especially thankful I don't have many stories of other peoples' penises, either. But there is one that comes to mind that is brief, and I think is pretty funny. It involves one of my best friends growing up, Steve McCallister. Steve was nine months older than me, and a proud member of the large McCallister family. Steve was one of the biggest and baddest individuals I knew. For now, I'll just say he was big, had experience at fighting, was quite good at it, and all of this made him somewhat dangerous. For the most part, he had a good temperament to go with these skills. Not always, but usually.

Now, for the most part, Steve worked for himself in some form of construction, usually with swimming pools, concrete, or masonry. For a brief time, though, I had gotten Steve a job with me doing commercial carpentry work. During this time, we didn't live too far apart, and I was picking him up in the mornings, and we rode to work together. It was during that time that this story takes place, for I know I was driving, Steve was my passenger, and it was in the morning, and traffic was pretty heavy. We were not too far out from Orlando.

I drove down a four-lane highway early in the morning. Steve spilled an entire large cup of very hot coffee on his groin. We're talking entire contents instantly dumped on his penis. Steve screamed and yelled, "Pull over, pull over!"

I looked for an opening in traffic and a place to pull over. Steve drew back an enormous fist and brought it even with my face.

"Now!" he screamed.

I realized the urgency of the situation—both his and now mine. I cut off people in traffic and whipped my truck to the side of the four-lane highway. Steve opened his door before my truck came to a complete stop. He jumped out and pulled his pants and underwear completely off in just a matter of seconds to escape the scalding coffee.

I was amazed at how quickly he was naked beside a four-lane highway. Because of the heavy traffic, there was some honking and a few shouts. Steve was unfazed. It was logical to him to be naked because this is what one did when one was confronted with this dilemma. I was laughing hard in my most heterosexual non-gay look I could muster for the passersby as I remained in the truck. No telling what people thought as they drove to work seeing a mid-twenties large naked man on the side of a four-lane highway. Steve was in no hurry to get dressed as he allowed his clothes to cool. I think he somewhat enjoyed exposing himself to a large number of people he didn't know and wouldn't ever see again. In a few moments, Steve put on his wet, stained pants. We both agreed it was no good for young heterosexual males to be riding down the road naked. After all, we were tough construction workers. We went to work.

THE MIAMI TRIP

At the time of this story, I was in my mid-twenties and lived a couple of miles outside of Oviedo. Steve McCallister lived in Oviedo about three miles up the road. Just prior to this, I had been living briefly in the only—at this time—apartment complex near Disney World. This apartment complex was located between Orlando and Kissimmee. I had worked in the Disney area for two years building a hotel. I finally got tired of the forty-mile one-way commute from the Chuluota area so I moved to that apartment complex to be nearer work. While living there, I met a woman, Marie, who also lived there and who became my girlfriend for two years. She did me and my ego a world of good. She was a very pretty stewardess, and she drove a BMW. Coming out of Chuluota, I had fairly low self-esteem. So, when a woman of this caliber saw something in a Chuluota heathen such as myself, it did me good. When the hotel job was winding down and nearing completion, I decided to move to the Oviedo area where the companies next job was nearing start up.

At one point, not long after my move, Marie's father passed away in Miami. She asked Steve and me if we could come to Miami and move her father's things from his barber shop and bring them back to the Orlando area, where she was living. She was willing to pay for our gas and get us a hotel room. It was the right thing for us to do, so we agreed. This was in the mid-eighties, and Miami was a pretty wild place with lots of crime, or so we heard on the news. I remember Steve and I agreed that we needed to take a pistol. I had a nine shot 22-caliber pistol that was fairly accurate. Steve had a 38-caliber pistol with no front sight. We opted to take Steve's. We figured we might not be able to hit anything with it, but at least it made more noise. We were hoping we wouldn't be needing it.

So off we went on a Saturday morning in Steve's older pick-up truck. The trip down was uneventful. We stayed the night in a hotel and met Marie and her mother, Mrs. Torelli, in downtown Miami the next morning.

Marie's father had been a barber in the same location for more than thirty years. So, his barber shop was right smack downtown up on the fourth floor of an old building. We were very glad her mother was there. She knew some of the other people in the building, and she spoke fluent Spanish. This was very necessary, for most of the people were Cuban and only spoke Spanish.

A few things stand out in my memory. First, on the bottom floor, street level, was a small grocery store. It was owned and run by a Cuban man. Marie's mother asked if we could park our truck in front of his store. This would be convenient since it was near the door at the bottom of the stairs that led up to the fourth-floor barber shop. There was no elevator in this old building. The grocery store owner in his broken English told Steve and me that we could park the truck there.

His exact words were, "Mr. Torelli very good man, I like a lot, you park truck right there. Anyone touch truck or your stuff, I blow their head right off. This true, they all know me. I blow their head right off."

Steve and I thought this sounded a little like something from the movie *Scarface*, but we were okay with it. He told us if we had things to throw away, to put them by the curb. The garbage truck would be coming on Monday.

Steve and I began bringing things down the flight of stairs from the fourth floor. Some of the barber shop things included boxes of combs, talcum powder, and small towels. We would set items like this on the curb. The Cuban store owner would say "You no want?" We were setting things there for the garbage pick-up because neither Marie, her mother, Steve nor I wanted them. The Cuban store owner would then go through the boxes and take anything he wanted. Then he'd put the rest back down on the curb for garbage pick-up. I remember Steve and I would go back up the stairs, grab another load of stuff, and come back down. By the time, we got back down, the things on the curb would be gone. We asked the store owner where the stuff was going. He said the street people were taking it. This continued the whole time, and Steve and I never saw anyone besides the store owner between our trips up and down the stairs. We were very glad the store owner was watching the stuff we were putting in the truck. Also, we were glad the street people apparently knew he'd blow their head right off if they touched the truck.

Another memorable thing about the move was the barber chairs. I knew barber chairs were capable of lying all the way back to the horizontal position. I always assumed they could do this because they were bolted to the floor. But, oh no. They can do this because the base of the chair is so damn heavy. It was everything Steve and I could do to get the heavy-as-hell chairs down four floors worth of stairs and into the back of the truck. We sure were glad we were going down the stairs as opposed to having to go up four floors of stairs. Steve and I were in our mid-twenties and in pretty good shape. We both agreed that if either one of us could have lifted just ten pounds less, we couldn't have moved the chairs.

So, that was about it for the loading of the truck and clearing her father's barber shop out. The truck was loaded, we said our goodbyes, and headed back towards Oviedo.

We had a couple of memorable experiences on the way back. Steve and I were both in fine moods, which was mostly because of our natural state of mind, and we'd done a good deed. Plus, we had gotten the hell out of Miami, and had started to consume beer. We cruised along I-95 headed home, and were driving through one of the longest, most desolate areas of Florida when we spotted this woman walking along the highway, going in the same direction as us. She wasn't hitchhiking, just walking. Steve and I knew this wasn't good, for in this area, she was miles from anywhere. So, after a quick discussion, we pulled over and backed all the way to where she was. From my open passenger side window, I asked her if she wanted a ride. She said she didn't and that she was fine.

"You don't know us, but I'm Mark, and this is my friend Steve," I told her. "We're really quite harmless, and you need to think about this. You're out in the middle of nowhere and miles from the nearest house or business. You can see that we have a truck full of barber stuff in the back. We've been helping a friend move their deceased father's barber things. We're not out cruising the roads looking for someone to kidnap. If you want, as much as I hate to, I'll slide over next to Steve, and you can sit by the door. That way, if we're to try anything, you'd at least have the option of jumping out of the door."

I guess my little speech, and hopefully, the good will we were emitting, convinced her to get in with us. Soon she realized we were harmless, and she relaxed. We even had her laughing. Come to find out, she had been riding in an air boat with her boyfriend and had gotten into an argument with him. He got mad, and he set her out on a small bridge on I-95 in the middle of nowhere. Some boyfriend. As the miles rolled by, I think it finally donned on her how far from anything she was. When we finally got to an exit, she said it was her exit.

We turned off the exit, and she told us we could let her off there, she didn't want to make us go out of our way. We told her, no big deal. Come to find out, she still had another six miles to go. We weren't about to let her off so far from home. I could tell she was reluctant to let us know where she lived, just on the outside chance we were trouble. So, I had what I thought was another brilliant idea. It was right up there with the having her sit by the door idea. I told her to have us take her all the way to her neighborhood, and we'd drop her off in the wrong driveway, or hell, for that matter, the right driveway. Either way, we'd never know the difference. She liked this idea, and this is what we did.

I think she finally realized how far from home she had been, and she couldn't have walked it. If she had tried, something bad sure could have happened to her. She gave us both a sincere thank you and a hug. I think she may have been a little shocked that a couple of mid-twenties, beer drinking, Chuluota heathens could give her a ride all the way home from the middle of nowhere and not try anything or ask for anything in return. We may have been a little shocked ourselves, but not too much. However, we thought it best not to let it be known among our male friends in and around the Chuluota area. We had an image to uphold and all of that, you know? Steve and I have what I call the damsel in distress gene. We go out of our way to help a woman. I have gotten in trouble a few times during my life because of this gene.

It was no big deal to us. It just seemed the right thing to do. Besides that, we were feeling good and just adding to our good deeds for the day. Can't have too many of those. It's to try and make up for all the crazy bad crap we'd done in life, along with trying to please the karma gods and all of that. We then headed back down the road to get onto I-95 to discover what adventure awaited us. We didn't have to wait long.

We were once again cruising on I-95 and driving through one of the long desolate areas, when suddenly we had a flat tire. No big deal since we had a spare tire and tools. The bad news was that the spare was a recap. For those who don't know, recaps were made for us poor people. Tiremakers just put a layer of good tread over a completely used-up tire. These tires sold for a fraction of the cost of a new tire. They had good traction, but were notorious for falling apart.

Back on the road again, we decided we'd buy a used tire at the first full service gas station we came to. It seemed like a good plan. We'd then have a pretty good tire and still have the recap for a spare. We hadn't gone very far when we heard a loud whop noise, as something hit the truck. We both looked back and saw a piece of rubber bouncing down the road behind us. Damn, the recap had started to break up. We both looked at one another with a this-isn't-good look. I think we shared many of those looks over the years, come to think about it. It wasn't too long, and we heard another loud whop, as another piece of tire flew off and hit the truck. Steve slowed down some hoping this would help. People sure weren't following us in our lane. We were going slower, and now we were leaving a debris trail of pieces of tire. For some reason, I was having visions of World War II airplanes being shot down along with Scotty's voice from Star Trek saying in his Irish accent, "I be giving her all I got, captain." We were maintaining our good mood and laughing about it. We reassured one another that we would make it to a gas station that sold tires just fine, trying to say this convincingly above nervous laughter. The talk was broken up periodically by the noise of flying rubber hitting the truck.

We finally did make it to an exit and pulled off. We went by a couple of places that sold gas but weren't full service gas stations that sold tires. As we limped a little further, lord and behold, there was a gas station that had a service area on the side. We saw tires. We pulled in. Life was good.

The place was a full-service gas station. It had about four gas pumps, and they would pump customers' gas. It also had a small store inside that sold drinks and snacks. They thankfully sold tires and did minor repairs on vehicles. The bad news was, there was only one guy working there on this Sunday. He was younger than Steve and I, only about eighteen. He was nice enough though, and we told him what we needed.

We needed two good used tires. One to replace the flat, and one to now replace the mostly disintegrated recap. He had what we needed. A deal was made and things were looking good. He proceeded to put our flat tire on a tire machine to take it off the rim. Steve and I told him we would help anyway we could so we could get back on the road. He said the owner wouldn't want us in the work area, for insurance reasons. However, he wasn't going to push the issue. We were a little older, friendly, fun, and we were drinking beer. Also, Steve was pretty big. The kid started working on the tire, but then a car pulled in, and he had to go pump gas. He came back and started working on the tire again, then another car pulled in. He left and went and pumped gas. Steve and I realized this might take a while.

I had taken two years of auto mechanics in high school. I didn't like mechanics and was really bad at it. I just took the classes because I thought I could work on my car while at school. The only problem was, I could never afford a car while in high school. I didn't get my first car until I was out of school. Anyway, I did remember how to use the tire machine to take off old tires. So, while the kid was pumping gas, Steve and I proceeded to use the machine to take off the old tire. The kid freaked a little when he came back and saw what we were doing. He calmed down pretty quickly when we explained he was busy, and he could see we knew what we were doing. Besides, did I mention that Steve is pretty damn big and can be persuasive? He did tell us not to let the customers see us drinking beer, though.

So now we were making some progress. The kid was doing the tire work if he wasn't pumping gas or attending the store. He started putting our new used tires on the rims with the tire machine. Now, this procedure is a little trickier than taking old tires off. I felt better letting the kid do it. He was trying to put our tires on, but now cars were constantly pulling in. After a while, I told him to keep working on the tires, and I'd pump gas, or we'd be there forever. I had worked at a gas station for about six months in high school when I was about fifteen. At this time, most people were still paying for gas with cash. I was getting pretty busy at the pumps. I was just putting money in my shirt pocket and making change for customers as needed out of that. The first break I got I went and gave the money to the kid. It was around eighty dollars. He looked at me and realized we were honest, not to mention cute and cuddly. My words, definitely not his. Things now were getting really busy for some reason. I was pumping gas and taking money, but if anyone wanted to pay with a credit card or get anything from the store, I'd have to go get the kid. I didn't want to be using the cash register and such. I'm sure the kid didn't want me to, either.

Things were busy, but we had everything humming right along. The kid and Steve worked on tires, and I handled gas pumps. The kid would run the store and credit cards when needed. I remember Steve pulled off to check a couples' oil, and he added two quarts of new oil. The kid rang them up. I couldn't believe the kid was supposed to handle all this business on his own. I think he was now glad we were there. We were taking care of business, laughing, and still managing to drink beer. Might as well, we weren't getting paid. We were just adding to our good mood.

Yes, indeed, things were going rather smoothly, then a truck pulled up. A guy got out and came toward us.

"What the hell is going on?" he barked.

"Can we help you?" Steve asked.

The guy proceeded to tell Steve that he owned the place. He wanted to know what Steve was doing working on the tire machine, and why I was pumping gas. He yelled at the kid for letting us do all of this and said something about insurance not covering us if we got hurt. We told him real quick, not to yell at the kid. He could yell at us if he wanted to. But not the kid. We told him things got real busy, and we just plain didn't give the kid a choice if we helped or not. Pretty soon, the owner settled down. Did I mention Steve is big and can have a dangerous look if needed?

"Okay, okay, you did what you had to, but now I'm here and me and the kid can handle it," he finally said.

We stood outside the garage area, drank our beer and watched.

It didn't take long before the place got real busy again. The kid would have to go into the store, ring people up, and do credit cards and other things inside the store. People waited at the gas pumps. Somebody pulled in with a radiator overheating. The owner tried to bounce back and forth for a while, but he was getting swamped. Steve and I looked at each other and said, "All right."

"I got the radiator," Steve told the owner.

I started pumping gas for people again. We were soon running fairly smoothly, but it was incredible the amount of people that were pulling in. Steve and I were checking peoples' oil and such, too. We changed an elder couples' tire for them. In the meantime, we kept telling the kid or owner to keep working on our truck tires.

Finally, I think it donned on the owner that we were way useful, and he was making money. We all stayed busy, but laughed as we reminded the owner to stay focused on our tires. I remember during all of this, an elderly couple pulled in and asked Steve if he could look at their air conditioner.

"We don't do air conditioners," Steve said.

He then politely told them they needed to go down the road another mile and a half, that there was a place that did air conditioner work there. Steve had no idea what was down the road. The owner was looking at Steve the whole time he was having the conversation. When the couple drove off, the owner told Steve, "We work on air conditioners."

I remember Steve never even looked at him as he started making his way to the tire machine and said, "Not today we don't."

Things finally slowed down, and we got our tires finished and on the truck. I'd like to think the owner gave us the tires or at least a big discount for our work, but I honestly no longer remember. I do recall we were all laughing and having a pretty good time. I think the owner may even have had a beer with us. I asked him, if we were ever in the area again and needed a job, would he hire us. He laughed and said that he probably wouldn't have much choice in the matter. I told him he was probably right, but he'd have a say so in our wage amount. Not much of a say so, but a say so nonetheless. We said our goodbyes and left.

The rest of the trip was uneventful. Just us going down the road drinking beer, reflecting on the day, and feeling good about ourselves. We made it back to Steve's and unloaded everything into his carport. I eventually got it all to Marie's and helped her sell it. That was the end of the Miami trip. I think from to time myself and fellow Chuluotians needed experiences like this. It allowed other people to see us in a different light and not just judge us on our looks. For I'm sure, a lot of the times we not only looked like just plain hippies but also kind of had a rough and tough look. We knew we had good hearts and were capable of doing good deeds, and it did us good when others could see that side of us as well.

RIGHT OUT OF THE MOVIES

When I wrote this story, I wasn't sure what to title it. It could be titled many things. Up to this point, I would like to think that all my stories have a degree of humor to them. This one really doesn't; unless you always see humor in the stupidity of the young. In which case, you may find some here. This story has all young people and some serious stupidity involved. But there was pride and revenge also at work and that can blind you to stupidity. especially when you're young. At least, that is one of my favorite excuses.

First, I want to tell a little more of Steve McCallister, so you get a better feel of how things unfolded. Steve is nine months older than me. We first met in Chuluota when I was five, and he was six. He was one of the eight McCallister siblings. I spent a lot of time with Steve and his entire family. It would be fair to say that all the McCallister family were quite athletic and full of pride. The boys especially were good at sports. These ingredients, along with a splash of meanness thrown in, made them very competitive and somewhat natural leaders.

Johnny, the oldest boy, played four years of college football as a middle linebacker. He was captain of the team his last two years and made all-American both of those years. Steve, who I ran with, just didn't handle school well. He got in lots of fights and partied hard. He quit school when he was sixteen. If Steve could have handled school and gone to college, I think he probably could have played pro football, because as good as his older brother was, Steve grew to be taller and a little bigger. Perhaps he was a little meaner at times, too. That one is a close call, though. Don't get me wrong, for the most part they were both fun-loving and good to be around. However, I have seen them both pick fights. I was always glad they liked me. In the hands of good coaches, Steve would have been awesome.

I'm painting this picture to give some background. We played many years of sandlot football, every Saturday, at ten o'clock. I was probably around eight when we started. When my brother and Johnny McCallister and a few others began playing high school football, they were also beginning to drive. So, we started going on the road and playing other towns. At this time, the young people in a lot of small towns were still playing pickup games of football and baseball. We started playing for two cases of beer for a wager. Steve and I and the others would have been as young as twelve when this practice started. Anyway, I always remember Johnny could really motivate people if needed. I could miss a tackle or let a guy catch a long pass, and Johnny would often yell and cuss at me until I felt really bad. But then he would turn things around and start telling me that I was better than that.

"Now go hit that son of bitch," he would yell.

End result, I'd find myself playing at a much higher level. Sometimes, I thought some of the guys played beyond their talent level and did some incredible things. I don't ever remember us losing any road games.

The closest town to Chuluota is Oviedo about five miles to the northwest. This is where we went to school. The next closest town is Bithlo, which is to the south about seven miles. Bithlo is in a different county, and the kids went to a different school. They also had different cops than us. The physical land elevation is a little lower than Chuluota, too. There were lots of pines, palmettos, and a few swamps thrown in, making land a little cheaper to buy. I think it attracted a little lower income level. There were more mobile homes there than in Chuluota. Now Chuluota for the most part had very small homes and low income families, but we at least thought we were a notch above Bithlo. I think it's human nature to think we are at least better than someone. Remember, most of us in Chuluota had it kind of rough at home, and we didn't have the highest self-esteem. This is how racism and prejudices of all sorts are formed. I think differently now.

We never went to Bithlo. A few times a couple of Bithlo people would come and hang out and swim in our main lake. But for the most part, there would be a mix of girls or babies with the males, so there were no problems that I ever remember. A couple of times, some Bithlo guys cruised by where we were hanging out, by the lake or the one store in town. We sometimes stared each other down or maybe exchanged a few words, but nothing more than that. There was never a need or a desire for us to go over to Bithlo, so we didn't. We'd pass through it sometimes if we were going to Cocoa Beach, but that was about it. So, I think Chuluota and Bithlo had low opinions of one another and considered themselves better than the other in all things.

Well, one day I got in from work late in the afternoon and went to the lake to hang out with the boys and drink beer like normal. There were a few people there, and they were talking of an incident that happened earlier that day. In our opinion, it was a very bad incident. It seems that while walking by our main lake and hangout area, Jack Hicks had gotten jumped and beat up by three or four guys from Bithlo. Now, Jack was the youngest of four brothers. He was about fourteen at the time. Their father was a preacher. The boys were pretty straight and religious. Only the oldest boy hung with us at all. But, he hung with us on a very limited basis.

So, here was this totally innocent young kid who gets beat up for merely walking by one of our hangouts and being wrongfully associated with it. I doubt if the kid had ever even swum at this lake. If it had been me or one of my peers, we would have taken the incident much better, for at least we were partying, hippie heathens, much like the guys that did the jumping. We may have retaliated, but maybe in a slower more thought-out way. Perhaps not.

What I do remember is Steve getting fired up and recruiting the troops. I liked to think of myself and a couple of my peers as some of the more logical and rational thinkers of our group. However, on this occasion we were all on the same page, and there was no hesitation to retaliate. So straight and religious were the kid and his brothers, that we didn't even consider asking them to join us. This jumping and beating hit us all as way wrong on all levels. Also, we had pride in where we were from. A lot of this came from sports, but a lot of it was just plain tradition handed down. So not only was it an attack on an innocent kid, but it was also an attack on our town.

With little thought, the Chuluota recruits, myself included, gathered at our lake early that evening. We loaded up in our mostly work trucks and headed to Bithlo. Our only plan was to see if we could find the three or four guys who were responsible for the jumping. We were going to convince them to go up against three or four of us of equal age, size, and temperament. Not much of a plan looking back. I did a head count before we left. There were seventeen of us. Three of whom were Ethan McCallister, the youngest McCallister, and two of his peer group. They would have been around fifteen at the time. There may have been a couple more of this age with us, I don't remember now. My group at the time was around nineteen years old, give or take a few years. Steve, I, and a couple of other longtime friends were building swimming pools at the time. So, a couple of the trucks were loaded down with tools and material for pool building. We had people riding in the back along with the mix. Here was our shabby caravan going down the road to Bithlo, consisting of about four trucks. I rode up front with Steve in one of the trucks.

We weren't really sure where to go. We didn't know where their young guys, like us, hung out. We went to the first convenience store we came to because in Chuluota, we either hung out at our one store or by the lake. We figured they might, too. The only people hanging outside the store were two girls around sixteen years of age. Steve and I got out and told them what had happened earlier in the day and why we were there. We asked where we might find the guys who were responsible for beating up the young kid. They told us some of the guys hung out at a nearby lake. They told us how to get there. I remember when they were talking to us, their eyes were dancing. They were getting excited. It was the kind of excitement that young girls get when they know something that no one else knows. They were busting to tell someone we were there. We were quite certain as we started driving to the nearby lake, that the girls were finding a phone and dialing the hell out of some phone numbers.

We drove down this isolated road where the girls had directed us. Shortly, we spotted the lake about two hundred yards from the road. We drove up to it. No one was there. We turned our trucks around and backed up to the lake so we faced the road. We shut off the engines, and everyone piled out. We talked about what to do next. We had a few options: wait there, continue looking, or go back home. It was a short conversation, though. As we were discussing options, two cars pulled in.

These cars stopped about one hundred yards from us, between us and the road we came in on. We couldn't see into the cars, and no one got out. We were taking this in when we noticed more head lights coming down the road. Suddenly, quite a few cars and trucks pulled in. Many of them left their headlights on as guys started piling out. The first two cars emptied out, too. Evidently, they had just been waiting for reinforcements. In the headlights, it was plain to see that most, if not all, of the guys were carrying clubs, pipes, chains, and other tools ready for a fight. One guy laid down across the hood of a car, and I assumed he had a rifle. Girls and young women piled out, too. They sat or stood on roofs of cars and trucks for a better vantage point. They were screaming and hollering. Damn, they'd brought their own cheerleaders. We had one woman with us. Her two brothers were with us. She had come with her current boyfriend, a big ole country rancher guy. He didn't hang out with us hippies, but we knew him from school. No telling what he thought he had gotten himself into. But he was standing beside us and upon seeing the Bithlo guys having weapons, he now had a bull whip in one hand. His father and big time rancher relatives probably would have killed us all for putting him at this scene. Just shows the power of women.

The scene was surreal, like something right out of the movies. It was a very dark night with lots of teenagers and young adults lit up by headlights. They were all holding weapons as far as I could see. One didn't have to be very smart to sum up the situation quickly. There was a lake at our back and cars and trucks blocking our only way out in the front. We couldn't escape even if we were willing to throw our pride away and try. They had us way out numbered, and we were in their town, so no way they could back down. I heard a little noise and saw movement behind me. I turned and looked and our guys were beginning to pull four-foot levels, shovels, various tools, and two-by-four boards off our work trucks to use for weapons. Anyone with any sense at all knew that some people were going to get seriously hurt, if not killed.

I did a quick head count on them. They had thirty-two and, like I said earlier, we had seventeen.

So, they had us nearly two to one. I turned to Steve.

"Let's go talk to these guys," I said. "Maybe we can talk them into forgetting the weapons, seeing how they have us nearly two to one. They should be able to beat the hell out of us."

Steve agreed. We hoped their pride and common sense would kick in, and so, this is what we did.

Now I don't want you to think I was in anyway heroic or in a leadership role. I'm sure my fellow Chuluotains would laugh at the notion. I was looking at the whole situation as crazy and getting worse. I couldn't see people getting so messed up and possibly dying. Steve was the leader, and I was just trying to be a voice of reason. I didn't want to get hit with a weapon, and I didn't want to hit anyone with a weapon. I knew I only had control over one of those two things, though.

Steve and I walked out from the trucks with nothing in our hands and stood in the headlights. Shortly, a muscular guy walked out from the crowd, wearing nothing but shorts. Come to find out he was supposed to be some kind of martial arts bad ass, the half-way leader of the locals. A couple of guys followed him. They stayed a few feet back and to the sides. They had clubs of various fashions. We told him what had happened earlier in the day, and that this was the reason we were there. He told us he knew nothing of it and countered that all this was happening because of something that had happened years before. We knew nothing of what the hell he was talking about. We also knew it didn't matter. Neither side could back down now.

"Look, you got us outnumbered, thirty-two to seventeen," I said. "You ought to be able to beat the hell out of us. How about everyone put down the weapons? No need for anyone to die over stupid shit."

The guy looked around, thought for a moment, and then he agreed. I'm sure he thought that he alone could take a few of us. I'm sure Steve had other plans about that, though.

A quick side note. I once saw Steve beat the hell out of a so-called martial arts bad ass. The bad ass had made this fancy 360-round house kick at Steve's head. Steve stepped back, and the guy's foot missed him. Steve then stepped back in and delivered a hard-straight punch to the guy's face. The guy dropped. Or more accurately, melted into the ground like the wicked witch of the West when Dorothy threw water on her in the *Wizard of Oz*. Steve knelt down and hit him a couple of more times. Then Steve proceeded to do one of the worst things he could have done while beating someone's ass. Steve began to talk to me and to the guy while still beating him. First, he told the guy he was a dumb ass for starting a fight with him, and he asked him if he now felt like a "getting your ass beat dumb ass." Steve also took time to explain things to me while beating the guy.

"You see, Mark, these karate guys always forget about how lethal the great American punch is. Then, when you get them on the ground, you have suddenly taken away ninety percent of their moves. What a dumb ass karate guy."

Steve beat and humiliated that guy. He had it coming though. He had started the fight, and he needed to learn some humility.

Now back to the story at hand. Their so-called leader agreed about the no weapons, because of us being far outnumbered and having some pride and some sense.

He turned to the guys behind him. "We don't need any weapons to take these guys. Tell everyone to put the weapons away."

Immediately, the guys right behind him protested.

"Oh hell no. I brought a club and I'm using it."

So much for his leadership role. He kind of shrugged his shoulders and said he tried. Steve offered for the two of them to settle the whole thing by just them fighting. But that didn't go very far.

We nodded at one another and backed away to our respective groups and told everyone what we'd talked about. It was just like being in the middle of a movie scene. We all knew there would be no backing down now and some serious injuries coming.

It was like watching a slow train wreck getting ready to happen and you're a part of it. One of my friends—I'll never tell who—walked up to me and asked what I was going to do.

"When they come running down here," I answered, "I'm going to try to blindside tackle some guy who has a club and take him to the ground and prevent them from hitting someone. I don't want to hit anyone with a weapon, and I don't want to be hit with one."

I knew there was not much of a chance of the latter happening. It wasn't much of a plan, but it was all I had. My friend told me he was going to run away. I smiled. I don't think the lake or his pride would have really let him.

I'm not sure what the others were feeling, but my feelings weren't of fear or bravery. I just had a sense of inevitability, a jumpy nervousness. I was amazed at how my world had changed drastically in a short period of time. I was standing in a field I had never been in before, surrounded by guys I grew up with, who were mostly armed with makeshift weapons. We were all staring across a lit-up field at lots of young guys who we didn't know, but who were intent on hurting us badly.

We stood out in front of our trucks waiting. There was not much else we could do. Our lone girl was sitting in her boyfriend's truck. Hopefully, she would be able to tell the story. Their girls were cheering and urging their guys on. Easy to do from the safety of a roof top and not being a participant. These guys were really going to have to come at us now. After a moment, their guys made some kind of cheer noise and came running toward us. A tension went across us, and some guys drew their weapons back to swing. Now much to my surprise, their guys pulled up about fifty feet away from us. Perhaps they were expecting us to run, or more likely, they just didn't want to be the first amongst us. Much safer to hold back until people were engaged and then come into the battle. Like I said earlier, we weren't overly brave, we just didn't have the option to fall back if we wanted to. But we sure didn't counter charge. We just held our ground. It let me know, though, that they weren't totally stupid. They knew some people were going to get seriously hurt and possibly killed. We also knew between the pride thing and their women cheerleaders urging them on, that they wouldn't be stopping a second time.

They regrouped, openly cussed us, and got their blood and courage up. They were fixing to make their second and final charge. All knew it was coming. Their women screamed and hollered in some kind of primal blood lust thing. Did I mention this scene was just unreal and forever etched in my mind?

Suddenly, a car came whipping into the field at a high rate of speed. Everyone turned to look. Then another car, and another, and another. It was four cop cars, and now they had their blue lights on. People scattered. Tools, two-by-fours, and people were being thrown into trucks. We were firing up and hauling ass. We had no desire to be arrested, and, yes, what a wonderful excuse to keep from getting seriously hurt. At this stage in our lives, cops weren't our friends and were to be avoided. But anyone who was there that night was glad to see the cops. If they were to say differently, they're extremely stupid or lying. The cops weren't stupid, either, and weren't taking any chances. They had waited until they had at least four cars before coming in. People and vehicles were now going in every direction.

Our small caravan had loaded up and blown across the field amongst the cops and Bithlo cars and trucks that were now leaving at high rates of speed. We headed out of Bithlo back to good old Chuluota. Shortly, two cop cars fell in behind us. Damn. Steve and I looked at one another with that all too familiar, this-ain't-good look. The cops seemed content with staying behind our caravan. As we approached the county line, we could see why they were content. There was a road block set up ahead, made up of our county cops. They had us all get out of our vehicles. Our Seminole County cops were in front, Orange County cops behind us. They told us they knew why we were in Bithlo. They told us if we went back, we'd be arrested. They also said they'd keep those guys from coming to Chuluota. We tried briefly to tell of the innocent kid getting beat up. They didn't want to hear it. We all agreed not to go back to Bithlo, and they let us go on our way without any more hassle. I feel quite certain none of us were eager to go back to a possible scene like the one we just left. Steve and I were now going down the road repeating, "Wow, how about that for a night?"

Looking back, I have a few thoughts. One is the unknown ripple effect. This was way prior to cell phones. Someone had to call the cops. Who? Perhaps someone who lived on the desolate road leading to the lake. But whoever called the cops may have saved lives. There is a good chance that whoever made the call has never known what damage that call prevented. I personally think it prevented a lot of grief. Many lives may have gone in different directions, or possibly ended, if that night had played out.

I've since read a lot of books on the Civil War. I read many accounts of how, after the war, some of the veterans were asked this same question. "During some of those battles how could you charge across an open field against overwhelming odds facing almost certain death?" Many of their answers were very similar: "It wasn't a matter of bravery. It was merely easier to go forward than to run."

Now in no way do I compare our experience with that of an armed battle of the Civil War. However, it did give me some insight into this way of thinking. It had become easier for both sides to go forward than to back down. I think all were damn glad to see the cops, except for those blood thirsty cheerleaders.

I don't know if the Chuluota kid who had been jumped and beat up ever even knew what had transpired for his sake. He might have heard, though, since it was a small town and all. But he and his family weren't in our circle, so they may not have known. Doesn't matter, we had to go, out of principle and town pride.

Right out of the movies, I tell you.

CHULUOTA TOUGH

"Right Out of the Movies" is the first story I wrote with very little humor. "Chuluota Tough" is the second, and it doesn't even take place in Chuluota. It took place in North Carolina and involves Johnny sometimes called John McCallister, the oldest McCallister boy. Humor or not, it is a story well worth telling.

Now as I mentioned, Johnny played four years of college football. He played middle linebacker and made All-American his last two years. So, he was tough and in shape, and he had that linebacker mentality. Johnny was about six feet tall and a solid 230 pounds. He was invited to try out for the Washington Redskins professional football team. However, Johnny had a pretty serious knee injury, and after playing organized football for eight years, four years of high school, and four years of college ball, Johnny retired from football.

After graduating college, Johnny went to work for an airline in North Carolina. This job required him to be at the airport very early. As a result, he often stopped around four-thirty at a convenience store to get a cup of coffee on the way to work.

One morning, Johnny once again stopped at a convenience store at his usual time. As he entered the store and walked past the front counter, he noticed a large black man behind the counter on the floor on his hands and knees. Johnny said he didn't think anything of it. Just thought the guy had probably spilled something and was cleaning it up. Johnny turned away from the counter and walked to the back of the store where the coffee was. In doing so, he walked past a large wooden tub near the front counter. This tub was full of ice and sixteen-ounce bottles of Pepsis.

He made it about halfway down an aisle leading to the back of the store, when, bam, something hit him hard in the back of his head. He staggered forward a few feet and then turned around. Upon turning around, bam, he got hit in the forehead with another sixteen-ounce Pepsi. The large man Johnny had seen behind the counter had gotten up off the floor and grabbed a couple of the sixteen-ounce bottles of Pepsi from the tub and had come up behind Johnny and threw them and hit him.

Now, if this had been me on the receiving end of the Pepsis, the story would now probably be over. But Johnny was tough. After getting hit the second time, he staggered back a few more feet trying to shake the developing cobwebs from his brain. His only thoughts were that he was being attacked, and he needed to fight back. He grabbed the first thing he could from the nearest store shelf to throw at his attacker. Damn. He looked in his hand, and he had grabbed a box of Captain Crunch cereal. Damn. He was in the cereal section. No good. Realizing this, he remembered he had a large ring of keys in his other hand. Johnny had a lot of keys on a ring for his job at the airport and for his father in-law's farm. Johnny threw these at his attacker, hitting him in the face and cutting him under his eye. The attacker staggered backward.

Johnny was a little dazed and wasn't sure what was going on, but he remembered he had an axe in his truck, and he was now going to kill this son of a bitch. So, when the guy staggered backwards after getting hit with the keys, Johnny took the opportunity to head for his truck. He ran out of the store and grabbed the truck's door handle so he could get the axe from behind the seat. When he lifted on the handle, he realized the door was locked, and he had just thrown his keys at the attacker.

He looked back at the store just in time to see a Pepsi bottle coming at his head. He jerked his head back just in time for the full Pepsi bottle to miss him and hit his truck door window, which shattered it. The guy had grabbed a few more bottles of Pepsi from the tub and came out of the store after Johnny, who now realized he could reach in through the broken truck window and unlock the door. He opened the door, reached behind the seat, and came up with the axe in his hands.

The very large man took one look at the axe, and the look in Johnny's eye and ran. I would have run, too. Johnny let him run and went back into the store.

There behind the counter, lying on the floor, was a young girl. The girl had been working at the store by herself. The big man had come into the store just prior to Johnny arriving. He punched the girl in the face and knocked her out. He had removed the money from the cash register and was dragging the girl to the back of the store when Johnny walked in. One can only wonder why the guy was dragging the unconscious girl into the back. When Johnny walked in, he only saw the guy, and he didn't see the girl.

Johnny called 911. Soon cops and paramedics arrived. The girl ended up being all right, physically, but was badly shaken up, as one could imagine. The cops did catch and arrest the guy shortly afterwards nearby. Johnny did good, very good.

I saw Johnny within a year of this happening. Of course, I had heard of it from his proud brothers, sisters, and mother. After hearing Johnny's version of the story, I said, "I bet that girl really loves you."

He just smiled and said, "Her parents still call me and thank me about once a month."

I'd like to think that Johnny's Chuluota upbringing played a small role in his being tough enough to help and possibly save that girl. His years of sand lot football, countless orange fights, and being drug down an old dirt road at night on a door pulled by a rope tied to a pickup truck (another story) played a small part.

Perhaps not. Who knows? Regardless, Johnny was tough enough to pull it off. It's a story worthy of repeating.

PICKING UP GRANNY

Johnny McCallister never left North Carolina. He went there to play football, met a woman in college and married her. She was from there, and the short version is, Johnny just stayed in North Carolina and still lives there to this day.

I'm not sure of the exact time table, but after some years of Johnny having moved there, a migration of McCallisters from Chuluota to North Carolina began. I had moved away from Chuluota by this time, so I didn't know all the details. I just know that Johnny's grandmother, mother, and at least two siblings, and an in-law followed him there.

I go to Chuluota a couple of times a year to visit a few relatives who still live there. Sometimes on these visits, I look up old friends who still live in the area. On one of these visits, I talked to one of these old friends to get caught up on the latest happenings.

"Did you hear Grandma McCallister died?" my friend asked.

I didn't know this, but I wasn't too surprised. She was up in years before I had moved away from Chuluota. Her husband had died quite a few years prior to my moving and was buried in the Chuluota Cemetery. I knew them fairly well. My friend smiled and said, "Yeah, she passed away up in North Carolina, and Gordon and Frida went and got her and brought her back."

"What do you mean they brought her back?" I asked.

Still smiling, he said, "Yeah, they loaded up their young son and daughter and took Gordon's pickup truck and went and got her. Made it a regular family outing they did."

Now, I didn't even know that was an option. That one could go get their dead relative and put them in the back of a pickup truck and bring them back home. Apparently, it was perfectly legal and perhaps still is. I had just never thought to ask. They drove to a funeral home in North Carolina, picked up Grandma McCallister and put her in the back of the truck. Drove her back to the Orlando area and dropped her off at a funeral home there. I would have loved to hear the conversations on picking her up and dropping her off. I can't imagine this is a common occurrence.

Shortly after dropping her off at the funeral home, a memorial service was held. Afterwards, she was buried in the Chuluota Cemetery next to her husband. It all made perfect sense and was the logical Chuluota thing to do. No big deal, nothing unusual going on here.

I've always had a couple of thoughts about this story. First, what a great way to immerse your young children into Chuluota culture and ways of thinking, not to mention giving them something interesting to share at school for show and tell time. Also, if Jeff Foxworthy ever got wind of this story, he'd have some new material. It'd be along the lines of, "You might be a redneck if you transport your dead granny in the back of a pick-up truck across four state lines."

Gordon didn't grow up in Chuluota or go to school with us. He was from a nearby rural area in a different county. While in his late teens, he met and began dating Frida McCallister. They married when they were young, had two children, and are still married to this day. His upbringing wasn't too far removed from ours, and he was thoroughly immersed in Chuluotaism with the Frida McCallister connection.

Gordon always seemed to me a super nice, fairly quiet guy who just went along with the flow. Even if that flow meant picking up your wife's dead grandmother and bringing her back across four state lines in the back of your pick-up truck. So, if he didn't originally have the Chuluota mentality, he sure gained it early on in life. If ever I had any doubt, it was erased at my own mother's funeral.

My mother was still living in Chuluota when she passed away in 1996. She was living alone at the time. She'd divorced her second husband many years prior. My brother and I were living in the Tallahassee area, and our sister lived in Seattle. We were all adults. Larry and I drove back to Chuluota, and our sister flew in from Seattle. We took care of funeral arrangements and all her other affairs.

The memorial service was held at a funeral home and was followed by a graveside service out at the Chuluota Cemetery. After leaving the funeral home, we had driven out to the cemetery approximately twenty miles away. We stood around waiting for the preacher, and everyone else to get there. I stood by my brother and sister when Gordon motioned for me to come to where he was. I walked over the twenty feet to where Gordon was standing.

Gordon said he was sorry about my mother's passing, then reached into his jacket pocket and pulled out a stack of photos. He proceeded to show me pictures of a big buck deer he had recently killed. He had the presence of mind to bring the pictures to my mother's funeral, for he knew I'd be there and thought I'd really appreciate this big buck he'd recently taken.

Gordon was showing me the pictures and telling me the story of how he had taken the deer. I was being polite, listening, and giving the expected compliments. I also needed to get back to the funeral, though, because the preacher had arrived along with everyone else, and they were waiting to get started. My sister kept looking over as I politely tried to get away.

My sister ended up walking over to see what I was doing, and to get me, for they were ready to get started. She looked down and saw the stack of photos Gordon was showing me. I think she was half expecting to see pictures of naked women instead of those pictures of the dead deer. She may have even understood the woman thing a little better. She didn't have the Chuluota experience that I did, nor did she understand the culture. I, on the other hand, wasn't surprised someone would take my mother's funeral as an opportunity to show me pictures of a deer they were proud of having recently taken.

My sister led me by the arm back to my proper place so the service could begin. I knew Gordon was one hundred percent Chuluotian, and I knew the culture. I turned back to Gordon and gave him a somewhat hidden thumbs up sign to congratulate him on his nice buck. Like Gordon, I was merely going with the flow.

THE LAKE SHARK

There are two movies I wish I had never watched—*The Exorcist* and *Jaws*. I was a teenager when I saw *The Exorcist*. It when I was right at fifteen years old, I believe, and I knew better than to watch this scary movie. For at the time I was living in what I always thought was a spooky house. The house always seemed very dark to me and just seemed to put off a bad vibe. The bad vibe may have come from some of the drunken craziness that went on there because of my mother and stepdad. I was often there alone much of the time. My mother and stepfather were gone lots of the time. Sometimes for days or more than a week at a time. They were partying with their World War II era friends while I was getting through the seventh through twelve grades at school unless it was summer than they may be gone even longer. It was a no-win situation for someone young. Scary to be by yourself in a spooky house, scary and sucky if your parents are drunk, screaming and sometimes violent. Many nights, I would escape and sleep on a friend's pool table. I was glad to be there. With this home environment, I knew better than to watch anything that might add scariness to the time I spent there. I knew better and never planned to watch this movie.

I made the mistake of getting into a car on a boring Friday night with a Chuluota friend and his girlfriend. They were on their way to a drive-in movie and asked if I wanted to go. We were half way there when they told me what movie we were going to see. I thought they were kidding. I didn't think anyone in their right mind would pay to see this scary movie. Perhaps they weren't in their right mind. They were from Chuluota, after all. I would have seriously gotten out of the car and hitchhiked home, if the drive-in movie theater wasn't located in a very rural area. I would have had a hard time finding a ride back home. I sure didn't feel like walking many miles on a Friday night. So, I watched the movie, and it stayed with me for a long time. But the second movie I shouldn't have watched, *Jaws*, stayed with me even longer.

I no longer remember the details of watching the movie *Jaws*, but I'm sure this was self-inflicted. In fact, I'm pretty sure I took a date to see this at a walk-in movie. It, too, stayed with me and thousands, if not millions, of other people for a very long time. Especially those of us living in Florida. Thank you, Steven Spielberg.

Pre-*Jaws* movie viewing, I would swim in the ocean with little thought. I would go out from shore quite a ways to swim, body surf, and enjoy the water in general. I even surfed for a very short period in my life. But the *Jaws* movie changed all of that. Post-*Jaws*, I no longer ventured very far from shore and was very jumpy in the water. If something bumped me in the leg, be it sea grass or a small fish, I tended to become unglued. There was a high risk of yelling or screaming, thus losing major cool points if there were women around. I wasn't alone in this way of thinking or behaving. Not all would admit it, though. I used to say that if Castro was serious about not wanting the people of Cuba to leave, he'd have made it mandatory for every Cuban citizen to watch the movie *Jaws*. That would have pretty much ended the attempts to cross over to Florida from Cuba in small boats, homemade rafts, and inner tubes.

This story takes place post-*Jaws* movie viewing. A couple of the guys from the generation behind ours—a few years younger—had gone to

New Smyrna Beach. They had gone the day before, stayed the night on the beach—a common practice back then—and had come back to Chuluota around noon the next day. Some of my friends and I were at the Lake Catherine beach area, a main hangout area for most of us, when these guys drove up after their stay on New Smyrna Beach. They opened the trunk of their car and pulled out a very dead and very stiff five-foot-long hammerhead shark. They had found it washed up on the shore of New Smyrna Beach that morning. Since they were young, male, and from Chuluota, they saw the way coolness of it, and loaded it up and brought it home.

After they pulled the shark out of the trunk, they showed it to various people. Showing the way coolness of it.

I suddenly had a thought. "Bring the shark down to water," I said.

We waded out into the water with the shark. I held the very stiff shark underwater, just enough where only the dorsal fin was sticking above the surface. It was a pretty impressive dorsal fin and looked rather menacing. I then pulled the shark backwards in the water and shoved the stiff shark as hard as I could forward with just its dorsal fin above the surface. The shark went fairly fast forward for about fifteen to twenty feet with just the dorsal fin exposed. Then it came to a slow stop and gently rolled over on its back and floated. Ummm, we'd discovered a new game.

We floated the shark over to a weedy area, just off to the side of the main sandy beach area, to keep it out of sight. We'd wait until someone new came to the lake and then wait for them to wade out into the water. It mattered not if we knew them. We'd ease over and get the shark. We'd hold it under water the whole time so it wouldn't be detected. We'd then maneuver ourselves within shark range of the unexpecting person, keeping their back to us. Then we'd allow the shark to float up just high enough so the dorsal fin was exposed. Then we'd shove the shark toward the unsuspecting person while a few of us yelled, "Look out!"

The swimmer would jerk around to see a rather large fin and shark slicing through the water towards them. Now, remember, this was post-*Jaws* movie viewing time, so most people had watched this movie and many screamed and made quite a scene. Not all, but many. The human mind did not have enough time to compute that there shouldn't be a shark in a freshwater lake, especially if they had recently watched the movie. Very similar to the mind not able to compute brick wallpaper being stretched across a dirt road at night.

This was high entertainment for a while. It probably was literally "high" entertainment, looking back. Eventually, there were no new targets, and our interest waned. Probably something new and shiny came along. The younger boys ended up leaving their shark on the shore of Lake Catherine, where many a people got to witness and enjoy its slow decay and very foul smell for three days. Finally, the buzzards got an opportunity to work it over and solved most of the problem.

In the re-telling of this story, it does give me somewhat clearer hindsight to why many of our local women didn't have a lot to do with us males. We were capable of doing a lot of stupid, stoned acts. We would often justify a lot of these stupid acts by saying, "Yeah, but at least we aren't breaking into houses or robbing people."

For the most part we weren't criminals, except for breaking the drug and drinking laws. Thus, in our minds, it gave us the green light to do many funny and stupid things.

COPS

My story wouldn't be complete if I didn't at least mention the cops in a couple of tales. For the most part, cops were simply to be plain avoided, if at all possible. Most of our encounters were from them pulling in to where we were hanging out at the lake or pulling us over on occasion if we were in vehicles. When I was growing up in Chuluota, having long hair was probable cause for being stopped and searched.

The cops very seldom found anything or any legal reason to arrest us. We prided ourselves on being able to spot cop cars a long ways off, even if they were in unmarked cars, and we would take proper steps if needed. Sometimes after searching us, and perhaps the vehicle, and not finding anything, they would still tell us that they were going to give us a break and not arrest anyone.

I remember I once made the mistake of pointing out to a cop that he had not found anything, and therefore, wasn't giving us a break, for we had not done anything to be arrested for. He didn't like that.

He got right in my face. "Son, the Sanford jail is fifteen miles away. Between here and there I will come up with something."

I knew instantly that he was right. It would be the word of a young, punk, hippie against a cop. At an early age, myself and others realized this. It saved us a lot of grief I'm sure, for knowing and acting accordingly, sometimes even going as far as thanking them for giving us a break when we hadn't done anything wrong. We did have our limits, though.

For the most part, we gave them the same respect they gave us. If they treated us decent, we treated them decent. I think we kind of looked at it as a game. If we were dumb enough to let them catch us with pot or underage drinking—the two most illegal things we were doing—that was our fault. We understood that they had a job to do. We weren't too high on their radar unless they were bored or just felt like screwing with us. Some of the cops knew us from them responding to domestic calls dealing with our parents and their craziness. A few may have cut us some slack for this, too.

Here's one quick story I remember that was typical of a couple of cops being bored and wanting to screw with us. A guy we knew had a van and had come into Chuluota. Two of my friends and I were riding around with him. A cop car got in behind us and pulled us over right about in the center of Chuluota on one of the main streets. What made this a little unusual was, there were two cops in the one car, and it was in the middle of the afternoon.

Probable cause for pulling us over was, we had long hair, and we were in a van. Vans were notoriously used by hippies in those days. They ordered us out of the van and searched all of us quite thoroughly, but didn't find anything. We're now standing on the side of the street in the middle of the day with our hair and clothing slightly tousled from being searched. A few older Chuluota citizens drove by and just knew we must be guilty of something, because neither they nor their friends ever got stopped and searched like we were being searched.

The cops then proceeded to throw everything out of the van onto the side of the street. There were bean bag chairs, a small 12-volt refrigerator, carpet that had been on the walls of the van, large speakers, and all the other stuff that van-owning hippies like to have. Of course, the cops didn't find anything.

"Well, there you go, boys," one of the cops said. "We're going to give you a break this time."

They then drove off, leaving us standing on the side of the street in the middle of the day with our tousled hair, disheveled clothes, and the van's contents scattered on the side of the street. The driver of the van calmly said, "Well, that sucked."

I thought to myself, "Yeah that pretty much sums it up."

I remember that none of us were particularly mad or upset. Just part of the game, it seemed. Sometimes the game sucked more than other times.

We had lots of encounters with the cops. Mostly because a lot of us had sucky home lives, and we hung out around the store and lake nearly every night. Cops in rural areas get bored at times, so they would pull in where we were and sometimes hassle us, sometimes merely talk. For the most part, these were not bad encounters. Most of the time, we knew we weren't doing anything illegal or had anything illegal on us that could be found. As I stated earlier, we could spot cops usually a long way off and hide things when needed, so some of the talks and encounters could be humorous and fun. Often times, we were pretty buzzed and fairly witty, as were the cops—not buzzed, but witty. If the cops were hard-assed, we would realize this and act accordingly to get them to move on. Most of the time, we could judge the kind of cop we were dealing with pretty quickly.

There was a time that a cop broke the mold and caught us off guard by his behavior. It was a late summer afternoon and about eight of us had driven out to some wooded property my mother owned right outside of Chuluota. We had ridden in either of three or four vehicles and had the vehicles parked in kind of a half circle. Most of us were around sixteen or seventeen years old. I remember this because I knew we were all juveniles, which can make a difference when dealing with the law. At this age, some of the guys had quit school and were now working, thus able to make money to buy cars, beer, and pot.

We had driven out there to smoke pot. It was a lot safer to smoke out there in the daytime than to be up around the lake hangout without the cover of darkness. We had never had a cop come out to my mother's wooded property. That was about to change.

Here we were sitting on the hoods of cars or leaning against the fenders in our half circle, bullshitting, quite stoned and having a good time in general. All of a sudden, a marked cop car bounced in on the small road onto my mother's property. We didn't spot him until he was one hundred yards out and closing fast. There was not much time to react. Two guys turned around with their backs facing the cop car, dropped bags of pot at their feet, and kicked them under the cars. Another friend pulled three joints from his shirt pocket and just threw them, scattering them on the ground, but kind of between all of us. This wasn't good. I knew the cop probably saw some of this activity.

The cop parked his car at the open end of our half circle. He opened his door and got out. He was a small, young man, and he wore a riot helmet. We'd never seen him before and had never seen a cop wearing a riot helmet before, except maybe on the TV news. We took this in and looked at one another. We were stoned, and we didn't want to laugh at the small cop in the riot helmet. Laughing at cops usually is not good.

He proceeded to ask what we were doing. We told him that we were just hanging out after work and shooting the breeze. He then asked for our names. When we told him, he checked them with a list that he had in his hand. He had apparently gotten a list of some of our names from cop headquarters, I guess to familiarize himself with who he might encounter, since he was new to the force and area. We didn't know that there was a list.

As he was going down the list of names, it dawned on all of us, that this cop hadn't gone and picked up the two bags of pot or the joints on the ground. He must not have seen any of that activity when he was driving up. So, the mood lightened up some, and now we realized that we were probably not in any, or much, trouble. Now, if he found anything, we'd deny any knowledge of it and figured it wouldn't hold up in court if he arrested anyone.

So, we felt better and started to kid with one another as the cop continued down his list of names. In our stoned minds, we were finding it humorous if one of our names was on the list or not. The cop wasn't really reacting to any of this, and he kept going down his list like it was a homework assignment. Then he came to Steve McCallister's name. Steve was the biggest and baddest of us. He'd been in quite a few fights by this time in his life. Steve, for the most part, was a likeable and humorous guy. He did, however, have a smartass side that could get him in trouble and in fights. Steve gave the cop his name.

The cop checked the list.

"Ah, yes, Mr. McCallister," the cop said. "See here you got in a little trouble last Friday night."

Steve and another one of our friends, Rex Turner, had gotten arrested the previous weekend. They had gotten in a fight with the owner and his employee at a place where you could pay to ride go-carts around a track. The cops got called, and Steve and Rex got arrested. I'm sure they were probably running their mouths, too.

Since they were sixteen and still juveniles, they were taken to the county detention center—a jail for the young. The cops left Rex in a large holding room and took Steve into a small adjoining room to question him. Leaving Steve handcuffed, they began asking him some questions. Steve, young and somewhat pissed off, and kind of a punk, had a bit of a smart mouth this particular night. Sometime during this interview, Steve told the big, black cop who had arrested him and who was doing the questioning, "Yeah, you're a bad man when you're wearing that badge."

Bad move. The cop's eyes got big; and he reached over and took the badge off his shirt. Still leaving Steve in handcuffs, he grabbed Steve and flung him across the desk. Then he proceeded to take Steve and bounced him off all the walls in the room for a couple of minutes. He more or less beat the hell out of Steve without actually hitting him. I'm sure this was an attempt to knock the smart-assedness out of Steve. It worked, too, at least for a couple of hours.

When they brought Steve out of the small room into the larger holding room, Rex was sitting there a little wide-eyed. He had heard all the noise coming out of the adjoining room where Steve had been. Steve was a little wide-eyed himself but much calmer.

"Tell them whatever they want to know," Steve told Rex. And then he smiled.

Rex smiled back and nodded. "No problem, no problem at all."

They both knew, there may be times when a guy can be a smart-ass, but this wasn't one of them.

This incident was what the cop with the riot helmet referred to, and it also showed Steve's frame of mind. I wouldn't say that Steve was pissed off about the arrest. He could see some humor in it. It was more like he just had a bad attitude about the whole affair. No one likes to get arrested and bounced off walls while handcuffed, even if they deserve it.

We were still trying to figure this new cop out. He was small, wearing a riot helmet, had driven onto my mother's property where we had never seen a cop before, and now he began to tease and taunt Steve about his arrest. We were not quite sure what his angle was.

After he had made a couple of comments on Steve's arrest, he asked Steve who the arresting officer was.

Steve, off handedly, said, "I'm not sure, some big ole nigger cop."

I think Steve used the N-word more to get a rise out of this cop than anything. Well, he got a rise. This small cop exploded.

"What!" he screamed. "What did you say? You mean Officer Owen? You're scum, you hear me, McCallister? You're scum of the earth. As far as I'm concerned you don't deserve to live. I will put you away, do you hear me? I will put you away for life."

He had spit flying from his mouth as he screamed, and he walked toward Steve. His hand went down to his side, and he grabbed his night stick or Billy club. Things had suddenly escalated.

The cop lifted that night stick about three inches up from its hanger on his belt. In unison, all of us who had been leaning back against the cars now leaned forward off the cars. This cop saw the movement and stopped dead in his tracks and backed up toward his car with his hand still on the night stick.

"Okay, okay, you got the numbers now, but there will be other times," he said.

We stood there taking it all in. Steve stood back and laughed.

"Life, you're going to put me away for life?" Steve asked. "For what?"

The cop walked backward all the way to his car door, opened it, got in, and drove off. We all were still quite stoned.

"What the hell was that?" I asked.

Now, I don't want you to perceive that we were threatening that cop with violence when we leaned off the cars. He sure perceived it that way, though. Then, and now, after all these years, I'm amazed how we all reacted the same way at the exact same time without words between us. It was more of an involuntary instinct that kicked in. I'm sure that we would have reacted similarly if any stranger in our midst had threatened one of us with a weapon. This one just happened to be a cop.

We found this stoned, Barney Fife, encounter quite humorous. We decided that we needed to gather all the pot and hide it better and leave for another spot. We didn't want to risk him calling for backup or start lobbing in teargas canisters amongst us.

Fortunately, this cop's time spent in Chuluota was to be very limited. He harassed us, and Steve, in particular, for only a couple of months. He made the mistake of pulling over some of the retired citizens of Chuluota and giving them a hard time. They promptly made some calls and got him transferred.

One more cop encounter story, then I'll call it quits for this book, but I do have others. This story takes place in Casselberry. Casselberry is a fairly small area that sits just outside of Orlando's city limits. It is incorporated and has its own police department. We hadn't any personal experience with them prior to this evening.

For the most part, we really tried to avoid small-time police departments. We tried to avoid all police, but the small-town ones, in particular. Lots of times, it seemed these cops had attitudes and would give us hard times if we had dealings with them. We thought these cops couldn't make the cut at bigger, better paying police departments, thus the attitude. Our thoughts at the time may have been wrong, but they were our thoughts.

In this particular story, there were five of us. Oz had borrowed his mother's car for the evening, and along with myself, Mickey Cox, Slim Richardson, and Jim Hicks, we decided to go to the big ABC Bar in Casselberry. We were around eighteen years old, which was the legal drinking age back then. I wasn't a big fan of this bar. They played mostly disco music for the dance floor. I was more of a rock and roll type of guy, but there were lots of girls there so I went.

We decided to smoke some pot while driving around before going into the bar. We were less likely to get caught driving around than with the five of us sitting in a car in a parking lot, or so we thought.

Now there is an unwritten rule, that when one is trying to avoid trouble with the police, the driver has the responsibility of looking for cops coming up from behind. We all kept an eye out, but the driver had the rear-view mirror, so ultimately it was his responsibility. We were all surprised when blue police lights began flashing right behind us. I was in the back seat and turned around and looked. The lights that were flashing were in the front grillwork of the police car. It was an unmarked police car.

An unmarked cop car, coupled with the darkness, meant Oz—the driver—and the rest of us had a good excuse for not seeing and identifying it. An excuse was not going to help, though. This was not good. Earlier in the day, Mickey had bought a bag of pot, but he was a novice, so he had a couple of us roll up his entire bag of pot into joints. We had two of those burning and had been passing them around when the lights started flashing.

The two joints got put out and either eaten or thrown out the window, I don't remember now. We unrolled all four windows, and Oz looked for a place to pull over. I remember smoke rolled out of the windows of the car like something out of a Cheech and Chong movie. Did I mention this wasn't good? Oz pulled over.

We had stopped on the side of a four-lane highway. The cop car pulled in behind us and two cops got out. Damn, two cops—this wasn't getting any better. One cop came up to the driver's window, and the other came over and stood by the passenger side of the car. Smoke was still coming out of the windows, but at least not quite as thick as before. Still not good. The cops told us all to get out of the car and to keep our hands where they could see them.

They had us all move over to the grass shoulder of the highway, away from traffic. The cop who had come up to the driver's side of the car proceeded to tell us, "Now boys, don't even try to lie to us. We have been behind your car for three miles and watching you smoke pot. We saw y'all passing the two joints around. In fact, you might want to keep an eye on the guy in the back passenger side. He's been double-hitting on you"—a slang term for taking two hits off a joint before passing it on.

We all looked at Jim and smiled. The situation had lightened up a little with this statement. We were stoned and still trying to assess the situation. Bottom line, we were caught.

One of the cops told us that because they saw us smoking pot, they were going to search the car. Right off the bat, they found a Frisbee underneath the driver's front seat. For those who don't know, Frisbees not only were a great recreational toy to be played with when one was stoned, but also, when flipped upside down, made for a great tray to clean seeds and stems out of marijuana. This particular Frisbee had lots of stems, seeds, and pot residue on it. Not good. The cop placed the Frisbee with its contents on the hood of the car. He told us that this is enough cause to arrest us all. The mood went back to being rather tense.

The cops didn't find anything else in the car. They then searched us. They didn't find anything on us until they got to Mickey. The cop found seventeen joints in Mickey's shirt pocket. Did I mention that Mickey was something of a pot novice?

"Son, what do we have here?" One of the cops held up the joints. "You really know we have more than enough to arrest you all."

"There's always one bad apple in the group ruining it for the rest," Jim said.

The cop turned to Jim and smiled. "Son, you have no room to talk. You're a double-hitter."

We all laughed, and agreed with the cop. The mood lightened again, and we're stoned. The situation was out of our control now, so what the hell.

The cop asked us what we are doing in Casselberry anyway. We told them that we were going to the ABC Bar. The cop with Mickey's seventeen joints in his hand said, "Look, it's still early in the evening. My partner and I do not feel like fooling with y'all. Besides, we would have difficulty fitting all of you in our car. We are going to give you a huge break and let you go this time. We would suggest you take your stoned selves back to Chuluota and stay out of Casselberry. We won't be giving you another break."

Meanwhile, as he said all of this, he put one of Mickey's joints on the hood of Oz's mother's car to his right. Then he placed another one about two-feet away to the left. He kept doing this while he talked until all seventeen joints are in two piles of eight two- feet apart. One joint remained in the middle. We all watched him work

When he wrapped up his lecture, he grabbed one of the piles of eight joints and handed them to his partner. He then picked up the other pile of eight joints and kept them in his hand. He told us again they were giving us a huge break and for us to go home. They then got into their unmarked cop car and drove off.

We were left standing, stoned on the side of the four-lane highway with one joint and a Frisbee full of the pot residue on the hood of the car. This truly was a big break and not like the fictional breaks cops gave us when we had not done anything wrong. I'm not sure what the cops were going to do with the sixteen joints they kept and divided up between themselves. I also know that it didn't matter. All of us could have been arrested, and Oz's mom's car towed and impounded, not to mention what we would have paid in court costs.

We took our remaining joint and headed back to Chuluota for the night. All of us saw the humor in the experience and knew the cops had won that round in the ongoing game. As we were going down the road, Mickey, who was sitting up front with Oz turned to Jim who was sitting in the back.

"Who you calling a bad apple, you double-hitter?" Mickey then lit up the last joint.

FINAL THOUGHTS

The time slot in history in which my peers and I found ourselves was different. In no way am I claiming it was better, worse, harder, or easier, than other times or generations, just different. Many of us came from broken homes, some very broken. Many of the adults in our lives were very self-absorbed and gave us little attention, supervision, or encouragement. Because of this, many of us young people found one another and helped each other survive. Thankfully, we chose to bury any pain and rejection with alcohol, pot, and humor. We could have made much worse choices to deal with our situations.

We were witnessing and living in the times of Woodstock, the Vietnam war, and the desegregation of the schools. We were too young to participate in Woodstock and Vietnam, but we sure saw and understood these things. The way our parents' generation for the most part were treating the Vietnam vets was just plain wrong. These veterans were our older friends and brothers. While it was not considered a real war by the older adults in our lives, we sure knew they were using real bullets and our friends and brothers were getting hurt and killed. They were guilty of nothing more than turning eighteen and being drafted. This knowledge was part of our attitudes.

I don't mean to whine, but the group I was running with sure felt we were getting dumped on by a lot of sources. Some of us had hellish home lives, the government and Nixon were lying to us, there were racial fights at school, teachers gave us hard times for not being good students, and all the while not knowing that our home lives were not conducive to doing homework and studying. Then there were our regular run-ins with the cops. Many of us didn't think we'd live past the age of thirty, and we planned, or more accurately didn't plan, our lives accordingly. Thankfully, we chose to bury ourselves with humor as opposed to acting out in violence or crime. It saved us a lot of grief and made for better stories.

I used to think there was a lot of talent wasted among the people I grew up with. As I have gotten older I have reconsidered this concept. I now see, that we can't all be pro athletes, musicians, actors, or comedians. Just helping your fellow brother or sister in your tribe survive difficult times may be much more worthwhile. So, it is not a waste of talent at all.

This is the end for this collection of short stories, though I have many others to tell. I want to see how well received they are and to give my friend, Sandy Tedder, a break from my constant asking for help with this work. I want her to once again resume enjoying retirement with her husband. If the voices of the past and the stories in my head do not remain silent, I will write again.

To the people of my first tribe, know this: if you or I were to find ourselves in need or danger, I have no doubt, we would all instinctively lean off the cars and be there for one another.

THE END

THANK YOU

Thank you for taking the time to read *We Lived It and Laughed- Tales of Chuluota, Florida.* If you enjoyed it, please consider posting a short review on the retail site where you purchased it. Reviews are very helpful to all authors. Also, tell your friends about it. Word of mouth is an author's best friend and much appreciated. Again, thank you.

~ Mark Perrin

ABOUT THE AUTHOR

Mark Perrin grew up in the small town of Chuluota in central Florida. He lived there from 1962 to 1985 and remained in that area for a few more years before moving to Wakulla County, Florida, near Crawfordville, in January 1988. The love of nature and history has been a constant in his life, and the area where he now lives is rich in both.

As a lover of history, he joined the local historical society shortly after moving to Wakulla County where he's been on the board of directors for many years. The thought of preserving a piece of history was one of the factors that led to the writing and recording of these stories for *We Lived It and Laughed*.

Mark Perrin operates a small home improvement business. The flexibility of this occupation allows him to pursue the hobbies he enjoys, such as hiking in the surrounding nature, fishing in local waters, searching for old bottles, and using a metal detector in his rural environment.

Made in United States
Orlando, FL
08 December 2023

40364086R00075